The Hidden Coast

The Hidden Coast

KAYAK EXPLORATIONS FROM ALASKA TO MEXICO

JOEL W. ROGERS

With a Foreword by John Dowd

Alaska Northwest Books™
Anchorage • Seattle

Library of Congress Cataloging-in-Publication Data
Rogers, Joel W., 1947-
    The hidden coast : kayak explorations from Alaska to Mexico / by Joel W. Rogers.
       p.   cm.
    Includes bibliographical references and index.
    ISBN 0-88240-403-2
    1. Sea kayaking—Pacific Coast (North America).   2. Pacific Coast (North America)—Description and travel. I. Title.
GV788.5.R64   1991
797.1'22'0979—dc20   90-45968
                                            CIP

Portions of this text first appeared in the following publications in slightly different form: "Orca: Johnstone Strait to Blackfish Sound, " in *Ocean Sports International,* March 1988; "The Translucent Sea: Baja and the Sea of Cortez," in *Alaskafest,* February 1982, and in *Backpacker,* January 1989.

Edited by Ellen Harkins Wheat
Book/cover design by Elizabeth Watson
Cartography by Karen G. Smith
Illustrations by Lawrence W. Duke
Photo editing by Carrie Seglin
Cover calligraphy by Glenn Yoshiyama

All photographs by the author.
Frontispiece: A July sunset on Clayoquot Sound, Vancouver Island, British Columbia.

Alaska Northwest Books™
A division of GTE Discovery Publications, Inc.
22026 20th Avenue S.E.
Bothell, WA 98021

Printed in Singapore

ACKNOWLEDGMENTS

◆

SEA KAYAKING, for me, is a life sport and a life-support system. Kayaking has provided me the opportunity to meet a unique community of people and to know them as mentors, friends, and fellow paddlers. To these people I dedicate *The Hidden Coast: Kayak Explorations from Alaska to Mexico.*

I want to thank Charley Fiala, Elliott Marks, David Arcese, Glen Sims, and Donn Leber for getting me started. Special appreciation goes to the kayak makers and their boats: Dan Ruuska and his Polaris II, Tom Derrer's Wind Dancer, Doug Simpson and Larry Zecchel for the Feathercraft, and Matt and Cam Broze for the Mariner II.

I am grateful to several persons for both encouraging my writing and photography as well as providing sources for my articles and pictures: Steve Wilson and Karen Hayden of *Entheos*, Bea and John Dowd of *Sea Kayaker* magazine, Carol Ostrom and Ross Anderson of *The Seattle Times*, Ed Reading of *Alaskafest* magazine, Charles Mauzy at AllStock, Larry Evans, Joe Crump, Sally Schwartz, and Sue Smith of *Outside* magazine, and Mike Wyatt of *Backpacker* magazine.

At Alaska Northwest Books, my thanks to both Maureen Zimmerman and Marlene Blessing for their ready acceptance of the book project, and to Carrie Seglin and Betty Watson for selecting the images and designing the layout. Ellen Wheat is the other author of *The Hidden Coast*—she edited this book and me as we went along. My thanks to her.

I'd especially like to thank my friend Sarah Shannon for her paddling, participation, and confidence in me, which helped create *The Hidden Coast*.

CONTENTS

❖

Preceding pages:
*As if a paddle
stroke would break
the spell, an
evening kayaker
sits motionless
in the Skagit River
estuary below
Mount Baker.*

Right:
*Kayaker-friendly
bull kelp, a sign of
deep water near
reefs and an
anchor if needed,
undulates beneath
the surface of
Johnstone Strait.*

FOREWORD

◆

As sea kayaking grows from the jealously guarded domain of a handful of eccentric individualists to a favored activity among a growing number of enthusiasts, so *The Hidden Coast* falls into place as an inspiration to paddlers and dreamers.

After reading Joel Rogers's book, it becomes clear why recreational sea kayaking took root on the West Coast. The area is ideal paddling country—from the ice-choked Alaskan lagoons to the scorched coast of Mexico, complete with dramatic history and a poignant, fragile present. This shore is home to some of the most spectacular wildlife on this planet, including orcas, grey whales, bears, and an abundance of bird species. Joel's book reminds me that although I've lived and paddled here for the past ten years, I needn't look beyond our own shores for exotic and extraordinary kayaking.

The book's most lasting contribution to sea kayaking, apart from the spotlight it plays on this beautiful shore, is its sustained enthusiasm for West Coast kayaking. It fired me up to get out there and visit the places mentioned, even when they were already familiar to me. Yet the book is almost as titillating for what it doesn't say as for what it does. Just swing the spotlight up or down the shore a few miles, and there's another inlet to explore or another wave-swept beach to wander.

When my son Dylan was seven, we flew into Hotspring Island in the Queen Charlotte Islands, then paddled along the shores of Lyell Island with its devastated, clearcut slopes. Dylan literally choked with astonished rage at the sight of the shattered forest. "Who said they could do that?" he asked indignantly.

For me, *The Hidden Coast* holds an implicit warning. Areas that we love to explore by kayak are on the edge of destruction. The beauty, peace, and wild splendor that Joel highlights are often just a chain-saw blade away from the big stumps of Lyell Island. By bringing these places to the attention of all paddlers and by encouraging kayakers to visit them, maybe such places will be saved. To answer Dylan's question, "We said they could do it by saying nothing." It is going to be harder for kayakers to say nothing now that "the hidden coast" has been revealed.

—*John Dowd, founding editor of* Sea Kayaker *magazine and author of* Sea Kayaking

ALASKA

CANADA

UNITED STATES

MEXICO

PACIFIC OCEAN

PRINCE WILLIAM SOUND, *Alaska*

CHICHAGOF ISLAND, *Alaska*

THE QUEEN CHARLOTTE ISLANDS, *British Columbia*

JOHNSTONE STRAIT, *British Columbia*

NOOTKA SOUND, *British Columbia*

SHI SHI BEACH, *Washington*

SKAGIT RIVER ESTUARY, *Washington*

WILLAPA BAY, *Washington*

COOS BAY, *Oregon*

PUNTA GORDA, *California*, HECETA HEAD, *Oregon*, CAPE MEARES, *Oregon*

SAN FRANCISCO BAY, *California*

CHANNEL ISLANDS, *California*

BAJA CALIFORNIA, *Mexico*

LA MANZANILLA, *Mexico*

The Hidden Coast

INTRODUCTION

◆

BEYOND THE TRAILHEADS and tidelines of the North American West Coast lies a remote, seldom-seen, marine landscape I have come to call the hidden coast. This edge between the familiar peopled environments and the immensity of the Pacific is a wilderness of secluded coves, offshore islands, sculpted sea stacks, and nutrient-rich estuaries known to all of us in the abstract, but intimately only to a few. These few are boaters, and especially sea kayakers—a new people of the coast, a returning human presence long absent from these shores, quietly paddling through a water world.

For thousands of years this thin, rich edge of the continent has been explored by the indigenous coast peoples in seaworthy boats. The Chumash of Southern California paddled twelve- to thirty-foot redwood planked boats called *tomols*. The native people of coastal Washington, British Columbia, and Southeast Alaska are famous for their finely crafted cedar dugout canoes. But it was the Aleuts of the Aleutian Islands as well as other peoples of the arctic regions who developed the skin boat or kayak.

Rarely will a people be identified for so singularly beautiful and practical a tool. Constructed from driftwood, bone, sinew, and sea mammal hide, the kayak evolved into a light, fleet, supple, sturdy, seagoing craft built to withstand the weather, make the open crossings, and navigate the intricacies of the shoreline. It is this legacy—the Aleut kayak, a vehicle born of necessity—that now returns reborn in the sport of sea kayaking.

The Pacific Northwest can be considered the heart of the renaissance of sea kayaking in North America. Oddly, the Northwest owes its popular love of kayaking in large part to the great Boeing Airplane Company layoffs of 1969 to 1970. There had been a community of sea-touring kayakers in the Seattle area, most notably the Washington Kayak Club founded by Harriet and Wolf Bauer and friends in 1948, and some talented local kayak designers and builders such as Ted Houk with his fiberglass Chinook and Skagit kayaks and Linc Hales's Bauer-designed Tyee series. But the sport stayed in infancy until the 1970s. The Boeing pink slips issued to engineers and avid whitewater paddlers Lee Moyer, Peter Kaupat, and Dan Ruuska spawned Pacific Water Sports, Easy Rider Canoe and Kayak Company, and Natural Designs. The first boats were whitewater kayaks, but by 1980 these companies, as well as Eddyline's Tom Derrer, Mariner's Broze brothers Matt and Cam, and Nimbus Ltd.'s Joe Matuska and Steve Schleicher in British Columbia all had production sea kayaks on the market.

Sea kayak tours began in the seventies with Alaska Discovery paddling Glacier Bay in 1972, the National Outdoor Leadership School Folbots cruising the east coast of Baja, and EcoSummer exploring Vancouver Island and the Queen Charlotte Islands.

New Zealander John Dowd settled in Vancouver and in 1980 founded EcoMarine, the all-purpose sea kayak store on Granville Island, and in the same year wrote *Sea Kayaking*, now considered the bible of sea kayak touring manuals. In 1984, Bea Dowd and John published the first issue of *Sea Kayaker* magazine, which quickly became required reading for all who are devotees of the sport.

By the early 1980s, kayaking was growing at an amazing rate; some estimate it doubled each year from 1980 through 1985. Anyone in the region with an affinity for the coasts could not help but have noticed the new sea kayaks lashed to the tops of cars heading off to Vancouver Island or the San Juans or even to Baja. Surveys revealed that these new kayakers conformed to a profile: more than seventy percent had four or more years of college, and they earned a median income of $45,000 per year. They were bird-watchers and environmentalists, ex-hikers and canoeists caught up in the energy of a new love—and sea kayaking can be just that.

In 1980, I had been paddling a canoe and living part of the year out in the Skagit River estuary, when a quick succession of events resulted in my acquiring my first kayak. The key was *The Starship and the Canoe* by Kenneth Brower, the first contemporary "cult" kayaking book, which in part tells of the life of George Dyson and his baidarkas. I was reading a copy while aboard the Alaska ferry when I met a party of sea kayakers returning from Glacier Bay. Their enthusiasm and character were wonderful, and engaged my curiosity. I disembarked in Seattle and a day later I was asked by Charley Fiala, the former director of the National Outdoor Leadership School's Baja branch, if I wanted to build a sea kayak and paddle Baja with him that winter. Without any hesitation, I said yes, and my love of sea kayaking began.

My first time paddling a kayak—the first few strokes away from the steadying hands of friends—was a deceptively simple beginning. The sensation of floating, the motion and glide through the water were intriguingly new. The inherent stability of the sea kayak, something all neophyte kayakers seem to discount, reassured me, releasing more energy and confidence. With my first steering stroke and correction, a course was set. A gentle learning curve began, and discoveries lay ahead that transcended the definition of a sport or the simple traveling from point to point.

Sea kayaking was instantly more than just going places in a little boat; it became a pathway toward understanding myself in the mirror of the wilderness, where my strengths and weaknesses are clear and present. The experience of place—the adventure of journeying to a new shore, the return to a familiar slough, the discovery of an ancient village site—gave substance to my life, creating a sense of belonging, of home ground.

The results of these journeys—the photographs, notes, and memories from the past ten years—have become the basis of *The Hidden Coast*. The kayak trips and expeditions in the book are as much about the character of this coast as they are about sea kayaking. The sport and the experiences seem to have become intertwined—the kayak being so indigenous to the environment it was created for. Perhaps that is the magic I am trying to describe. If there was one clear objective in my photography and writing for this book, it was to tell of the richness and reward of knowing these coasts from the cockpit of a sea kayak.

The Hidden Coast was written for the lovers of coasts, for the ones who wonder where these slender little boats might take them. And it is written especially for those who have already paddled beyond the fringe of civilization. More than anything else, it is an affirmation of why we sea kayak.

The Hidden Coast

OIL TO ICE

◆

Prince William Sound

Never in the millennium of our
tradition have we thought it possible
for the water to die.
—Walter Meganack
Chief of the native village of Port Graham

THE BRIGHT ORANGE shapes separate and coalesce, vibrant and foreign against the slate-grey, forest-green coast of Knight Island. As our boat closes the distance, the shapes become individuals—biologists and bureaucrats—fresh from their helicopter, bulky in their fluorescent survival suits. They walk the beach, some taking notes. Others, their feet toeing the cobbles, gather to study a freshly dug pothole rapidly filling with crude oil.

It is a clear, calm afternoon on the third of May 1990, thirteen months after the tanker *Exxon Valdez* rode her hull over Bligh Reef, rupturing eight of her thirteen cargo compartments and releasing 10.8 million gallons of Alaska crude oil into Prince William Sound. Throughout the spring of 1989, the same winds, tides, and currents that naturally flush and feed this secluded part

Left: Brash ice, low clouds, tidewater glaciers. Water dominates the land at Barry Arm, Prince William Sound.

C H U G A C H   R A N G E

ALASKA

Coxe Glacier
Barry Glacier
Cascade Glacier

College Fjord

•Valdez

Barry Arm

Harriman Fjord

Pt.
Doran

Hobo Bay

Port Wells

Bligh Reef

Whittier•

Wells Passage

Prince William Sound

•Cordova

Bay of Isles

Knight Island

Copper Bay

GULF OF ALASKA

· OIL TO ICE ·

PRINCE WILLIAM SOUND

PACIFIC OCEAN

N

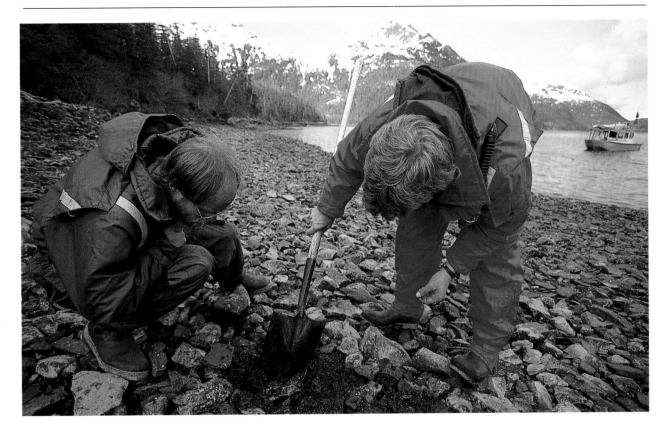

♦

Spring and the oil spill assessment teams return to the Bay of Isles, one winter after the Exxon Valdez oil spill.

of Alaska drove the slick with fateful randomness. The oil smothered the life on one beach, missed an adjacent bay, and turned with the ebb to consume another island, another shore in a silent, glistening creep.

In its westward course, the oil slick traveled thirty-five miles in seven days to foul the east end of Knight Island, invading the Bay of Isles and smothering the beach this assessment team now walks with tons of oil.

The men eye our boat with surprise. Our kayaks stowed atop the wheelhouse, we look like the return of the wilderness tourists. But we, too, are making our own assessments. I go ashore with my cameras to photograph, beginning a document of both the aftermath of the spill and the places it left untouched. Perry and Lois Solmonson, with their good ship *Kayak Express*, are here to check the condition of the beaches, so they will

be able to answer the many questions their clients will have in a week when the Solmonsons begin their first full season shuttling kayakers throughout the sound.

The year before, Perry had prepared the *Kayak Express* for kayakers. But he, like many other maritime Alaskans, ended up shuttling Exxon crews instead; he ran the *Express* on contract between the cleanup sites on Knight, Smith, and Naked islands. We return to the same sites that the previous summer had been choked with boats and barges, floating dorms and landing craft. All that now remains is an occasional oil boom and a pervasive quiet.

Perry at first was surprised how clean the beaches appear, after time, tide, and the roughneck energy of winter have scoured the intertidal. On the surface, the sound looks normal. We hope it has made a rapid recovery. But the pothole at the Bay of Isles has destroyed our optimism. The oil is not gone, just less visible, harder to get at. It has saturated the basement sands.

In the summer of 1986, I had paddled Prince William Sound on a route just north of here, through Culross Passage to Eshamy Bay and Knight Island Passage. It was July. Salmon crowded the bays and streams; resident ducks, seabirds, eagles, and otters were occupied with young. The habitat was rich and healthy. May 1990, in contrast, screams with silence: there are few birds, even fewer otters. Nothing is moving along the beach, across the sky, upon the surface throughout the Bay of Isles.

The biologists' work complete, the assessment team returns to its helicopter. As I pack my cameras away, an unmistakable high-pitched call brings me around. A mature bald eagle is perched in a spruce tree not more than 100 yards away. But my relief at seeing something so remarkable, living, is quelled by the oil staining the magnificent bird's head feathers. He stares back, and I retreat, knowing that this bird is dying. For a moment, the enormity of the *Exxon Valdez* disaster becomes personal and focused, as unavoidable as the piercing cry of this one eagle.

When the world learned of the *Exxon* spill, it began to learn about Prince William Sound as well. Continually, the media accounts spoke of this little-known "pristine," "natural" environment tucked up into the northeast corner of the Gulf of Alaska. Larger than Vancouver Island, Prince William Sound is its own geographic entity, isolated from the Alaskan interior, from Anchorage and Fairbanks, by the massive wall of peaks and ice fields known as the Chugach Range. To the south, it is sheltered from the Pacific Ocean by a barrier of slender, glaciated islands—Latouche, Montague, Hinchinbrook, and Hawkins. Within lie 15,000 square miles of calm waters, perfect mountains, and convoluted shorelines still emerging from the recession of the glaciers some 15,000 to 12,000 years ago.

It has only been a thousand years since the first people, the Koniag—the Eskimos from Kodiak Island—kayaked into the sound and settled there. Two hundred years ago, the Russians and Americans began harvesting Prince William Sound's estimated 200,000 sea otters to near extinction. John Muir and E. W. Harriman discovered Harriman Fjord 100 years later, publicizing to the nation the natural beauty of the sound. During the World War II era, the military punched a rail line through the Chugach Mountains from Anchorage to Whittier, opening the sound to deep-sea shipping. And in 1977, the first of over 9,000 tankers loaded with North Slope crude oil set sail from Valdez.

Today, Prince William Sound is no longer pristine, no longer isolated. It faces proposed timber clearcuts, new recreational development, and dwindling salmon stocks, and it is still threatened by another oil spill. The sound struggles to recover its former richness. Yet, in spite of the collective indignities that the sound has suffered, it is still one of the most beautiful and rewarding kayaking destinations in the world.

I refold the USGS quadrangle to display my intended paddling route and fit the map into a ziplock bag. Next, clothes: I pack fast, weeding out what I won't need, separating what I'll wear paddling from what I'll need ashore. Through the wheelhouse windows, I can see the broad strait called Port Wells which stretches east to the glaciers and mountains of College and Harriman fjords. As the *Express* speeds to my dropoff point, I glance up the strait with anticipation. I tuck thirty rolls of film into a dry bag, enough for six days, and set it aside.

Entering Wells Passage, we cross into the waters missed by the *Exxon Valdez*, leaving behind the three days I had traveled aboard the *Kayak Express* and explored the wild coves and oiled beaches along much of western Prince William's coast. Now the stain of the oil spill, the memory of the damage, and the undetermined legacy can be tucked away, assimilated into the

◆

Right: First to shake the burden of snow, an islet on the north shore of Port Wells greens in the midday sun.

In the lingering
spring twilight of
Alaska, kayaks are
tethered for the
night on Copper
Bay, Knight Island.

reverie of my own experience kayaking Prince William Sound.

At a small cove northeast of Pigot Point, we slide my kayak off the stern, fully loaded. Lois hands me down a sandwich, and I push off. The *Kayak Express* turns toward Whittier, twelve miles distant. Perry waves, and a moment later they're gone.

My boat for this trip is an aqua Wind Dancer, and it's loaded to the gills. I set my spray skirt tight and leave the rudder up. Using my body and paddle to steer, I follow the curve of the shoreline, warming up, taking my time to get up to speed. There is no wind and a negligible current. The sun above is slowly being overrun by a textbook 1,004-millibar low-pressure system. In this part of the country that means rain for the rest of the trip. This is no foreboding; it's more a fact of life when kayaking Prince William Sound. Perry had talked about the rain as a rite of passage: "You need three tarps: one for the kitchen, one close over your tent, and another inside as an extra floor. When it really gets bad, tarp your clothesline. And make sure you take an umbrella to stay dry when you leave the tent at night."

My umbrella lies ready beside my seat. Nearby Whittier, with an average of 189 inches of precipitation per year (including twenty-one feet of snow), garners respect from a Seattle native. But this low will take its time.

I enter four-mile-wide, ten-mile-long Port Wells and see the far distant entrances to College and Harriman fjords dwarfed by the Chugach massif that rises up out of the sound in the excessive scale of Alaska. In 1902, John Muir wrote about the Chugach Range: "Peak over peak dipping deep in the sky, a thousand of them, icy and shining, rising higher, higher beyond and yet beyond one another, burning bright in the afternoon light."

It is as Muir wrote, near countless peaks, nameless beautiful horns rising to shoulder the great summits—Mount Valhalla, 12,135 feet, Mount Goode, 10,610 feet, and Marcus Baker, 13,176 feet—spawning glaciers in all directions, some winding and falling with frozen inertia into the jade waters of my intended goal, Harriman Fjord. As I paddle toward them, I watch the leading edge of the front wedging over their summits. It blocks the sun until the only color remaining throughout Port Wells is the ethereal turquoise of the distant glacier ice.

Hobo Bay is my first camp. One of a series of bays along the west side of Port Wells, its still water stretches back like a purse into a rounded, steep-sided alpine valley. At its head, a remnant of the glacier that long ago created this soft-edged landscape straddles the ridge. The glacier's onetime terminal moraine sprawls, stranded by the receding ice and isolated by the advancing sea—an arc of earth created by the then bulldozerlike advance of the glacier. Shaped like a spit, the moraine nearly closes off the bay, creating an easy-landing, two-sided, shale beach camp at its point.

I site my tent along the beach margin where the forest begins. The kitchen goes out on the spit's end, where a forested would-be islet provides some protection from the threatening weather. While I hurry to get the stove going, I wonder about the approaching front, the possibility of high wind, the height of the tide, and bears. I make a mental note to tie up the kayak, even though it's resting in the beach grasses well above my tent—I've seen kayaks and tents blow away. The assorted potential problems and logical solutions dwindle in my mind as dinner heats. I find a perfect seat beneath the boughs of a western hemlock and anticipate food, happy in my solitude.

Rain sounds, crows in the trees, periodic cries of eagles, and along the shore, the cackling of harlequin ducks pairing up. It's probably past sunrise, somewhere between 5:00 and 6:00 A.M. There are low clouds, no wind, and it's cold. Bergy bits, the term for small icebergs, drift seaward in the distance. The rain, a steady drizzle, is amplified against the tent fly. I turn from the flap and check the corners of my old dome tent for seepage: dry enough. My mind weighs the options:

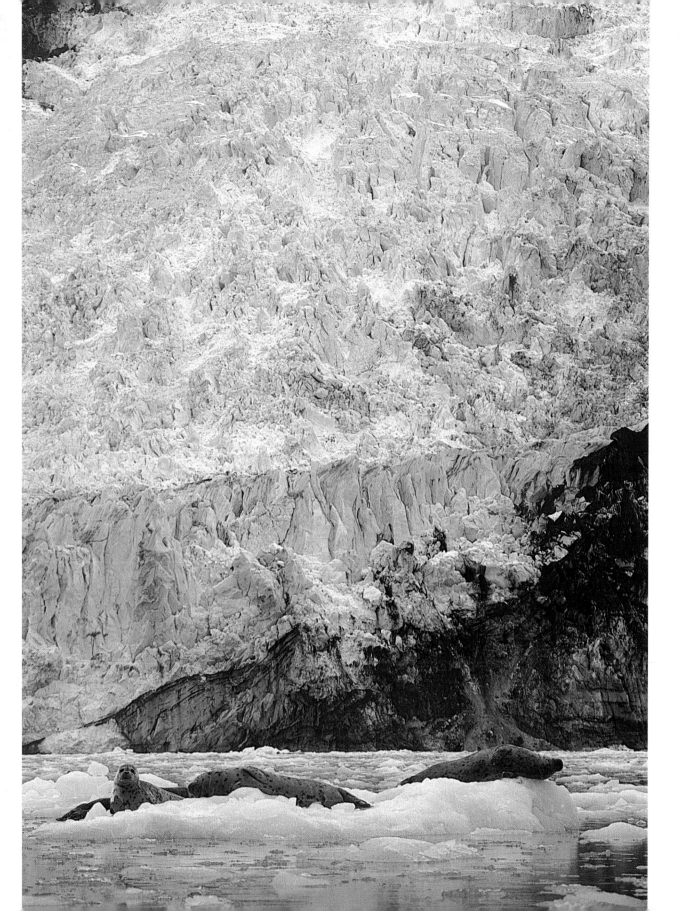

◆

Harbor seals warm themselves atop ice floes beneath the terminal moraine of the Cascade Glacier, Barry Arm.

Overleaf: Paddling through a mirror image, sea kayakers pass beneath the mountains rising out of Copper Bay, north coast of Knight Island.

I'm roughly eight miles inside Port Wells and ten miles from the first of the great tidewater glaciers. I can break camp now and paddle well into the fjords, wait out the rain over breakfast, or burrow back into my sleeping bag.

Grape Nuts or granola? I walk into the relative dryness of the forest after my cached food bag, flushing crows and shaking the raindrops off the snowberry bushes. Amidst the noise of cloth against branch I think I hear a whale sounding—an orca or a humpback. Quickly I backtrack to the beach and wait, scanning about a mile out. Nothing. Grape Nuts it is, beneath the trees.

As I crunch my way through breakfast, I am witness to the morning patterns of the local waterfowl. Grebes I have to identify in the bird book (red-necked); they fish in ten to fifteen feet of water forty feet offshore. The harlequins, five of them, want to feed along the edge of my fine gravel beach, but hang back, arguing about the threat of my presence. They are safe from me, safe from the oil: Port Wells was spared. It is Prince William Sound just as it should be.

My somewhat abstract gaze falls on something that does not register at first. I am conscious of the movement of two, now three, black shapes rising out of the water near shore. They are dorsal fins—orcas! A whoosh of air, plumes of mist, and the dorsal fins slide beneath the surface. Two females and a young one travel through the space where the grebes have been, roiling the cold waters in their passing with an implicit power that electrifies my simple morning. The pod surfaces again in the same order of appearance: two then one, along the shore edge. I hear their breaths once more, and then my front yard is returned to the smaller if no less important activities of harlequins and grebes.

I return to my coffee, my apropos copy of Melville's *Moby Dick*, and my satisfaction with Hobo Bay. As morning stretches into afternoon, Ishmael signs on, the tide comes and goes, and the rain softens whatever resolve I have to move on.

The following morning is a travel day. Amidst the activity of packing the boat, it's just luck that I am momentarily still when four miles off, clear across Port Wells, comes the faint sound of whales—orcas breathing, two then one. Listening again to make sure, I am intensely pleased to recognize the small pod of the morning before, now traveling along the opposite shore, heading west. I wonder where they've been, if they've traveled and hunted the entire shoreline of both fjords. Just my recognizing them and sensing their possible behavior creates within me a remarkable feeling of kinship. I find myself thinking of them as survivors, glad they had the good fortune or presence of mind to avoid the oil spill.

I paddle into winter. Snow covers all the peaks and hills within view. Snow, in fact, covers everything down to the tideline. Well down Barry Arm, the entrance to Harriman Fjord, the waters surrounding my kayak are increasingly littered with ice: bergy bits (as big as a small house), growlers (larger than six feet across and no more than three feet above water), and brash ice (fragments no bigger than a refrigerator) crowd my path. The rain lightens and I push back my hood, opening up my peripheral vision. I drop the rudder and begin navigating cautiously through the jewel-like clutter, taking care not to chip the boat's Gel-coat.

May 5 is an early start for tourist season at Prince William Sound, but then the time to visit depends upon what you want to experience. Early May means no wildflowers, no bugs, no people, no suntan—just orcas, migrant waterfowl, glaciers, and rain. Snug beneath my hood, hands warm within kayaker's pogies, I am content with my decision to come early, to see the fjords in the final moments of winter.

At Point Doran, Harriman Fjord opens, revealing glaciers winding down from the clouds. I paddle through the thick of a great stream of ice flowing from the calving glaciers of Barry Arm, picking my way to the eastern shore like an ice breaker searching for leads. Three glaciers calve into the arm: Cascade, Barry, and Coxe.

Together they form an almost unbroken ice face 150 feet high and one mile across. I drift to a stop at the crack of a serac the equivalent of a twelve-story building breaking off from the ice face. It tumbles like a fainting soldier into the bay, creating a ground swell that rears up in a ponderous wave. The wave makes its way toward me, its energy blunted by all the floating ice. I stay still, away from any of the larger, potentially unstable bergy bits as the wave passes beneath my kayak and rebounds off the shore.

Minute by minute, the sudden report and rumbling thunder of ice falling into the sea reverberates off the mountain walls that enclose Barry Arm. It is an intimidating world, cold and seemingly inhospitable until I begin to pass a remarkable assortment of residents comfortable within this ice amphitheater. The grey lumps loafing on bergy bits are harbor seals; the brown ones are sea otters. Overhead, black-legged kittiwakes wheel and call, while serious territorial discussions take place between black oystercatchers along the tideline.

Matching the natural features of the landscape with the quadrangle, I find a campsite. To the right of Coxe Glacier is a small point of land, just clear of the glacier's steeply sloping face. I beach beside the tracks of a foraging river otter, and pull the boat high.

My time at Barry Arm is spent sitting on a rock grandstand just watching the glaciers. At times I catch a seal watching me, and as I turn it slips beneath the surface. From my perch beneath my umbrella, I take notes and pictures, and I watch the calving ice and curious seals. I have become a resident more than an intruder.

Deep in this pocket of wilderness, I seem to be accepted. My kayak and I move as the Koniag once did. The otters eye me from ice floes, sliding into the sea as their natural caution overcomes their intense curiosity; they seek protection but without any sign of alarm. The otters' nonchalance is curious: is it because few people come here, at this time of year? Possibly I'm not recognized as a man but a floating, long and pointy living thing with thin wings? Occasionally, I have to speak to let a dozing otter know I'm near so I won't startle it.

Days later I pack the Wind Dancer a last time for the return to Whittier. I have over twenty miles to paddle with the outgoing tide. I sort through the cockpit day bag and hesitate over the sunglasses. Maybe today they'll get some use.

The glaciers were busy overnight: the bay is full of ice, there is no open water. I clunk my way slowly through the slurry. For miles, I rudder and lean, reach out to fend off the bigger chunks, paddle briefly and fend again, the otters watching me go. Just short of Point Doran, I break clear and paddle as fast as I can.

I keep the pace until I sweat, covering a mile in a few minutes before settling into a daylong rhythm. I am paddling back into spring, passing rafts of ducks—oldsquaw, shovelers, and scoters. A flock of extra-large shorebirds sends me diving again for the bird book. Whimbrel.

Along the forest margin, varied thrushes, orange against the green, remind me of the biologists and the spill. I'm left wondering if we will ever know the total devastation of the *Exxon Valdez* incident, measured not just in wildlife losses and the degradation of the sound but in our own failure to save this great resource. And now, in the aftermath, we witness the degeneration of our conviction as the horror of this disaster dissipates from headlines and memories.

In the fall of 1990, the legacy of the Prince William Sound oil spill is a residue of legal entanglements and political compromise. Meanwhile the moment of this tragedy is passing and with it the momentum for industry, the states, the federal government, and the people to forge a collective attitude and an effective technology to prevent the further destruction of our environment.

As I pass Point Doran, the rain stops completely. By Hobo Bay, I paddle into the sunshine with no regrets for my time spent in the introspective tenor of the rain. But try as I may I can't shake the simple question: when will the glistening oil come again?

GOING OUTSIDE

◆

Chichagof Island

NOWHERE ELSE WILL you find more idiosyncratic machines. Dotted throughout the northern land-scape—tinkered, tweaked, and forever welded into some form of running order—machines in Alaska tend to have their own personae, their own oil-dripping charac-ter. Bought used, jury-rigged, and worked to exhaustion, they rest wherever they lose their usefulness, only to be reborn again for some purpose their original designers never dreamed of. Until one day they stop for good, oxidizing in a ring of fireweed, monuments to the only land that could master them.

Like the people of Alaska, their machines are anachronisms. They are too hardy, too individualistic to make it in the Lower 48. Huge D-9 Cats bulldoze about Fairbanks like latter-day musk-oxen. Along the Beaufort seacoast, the startling forms of arctic drill rigs, coated in hoarfrost, rise up from the tundra like modern totems.

But of all the truly wondrous machines in the North, it is the bush planes that universally capture Alaskans' hearts. Their plodding, droning progress

Left: In the early morning, kayaks glide quickly enough to create a breeze, quietly enough to hear the working of the boat frames. Chichagof Island, Southeast Alaska.

29

Gustavus

Juneau

Icy Strait

Cape Spencer

Hoonah

Chichagof

Yakobi
Island

Island

Chatham Strait

PACIFIC OCEAN

WHITE SULPHUR HOT SPRINGS

Dry Pass

Ogden Passage

▲DOOLTH MOUNTAIN

Klag Bay

Myriad Islands

Inside Passage

Granite Islands

Vorota Island

ALASKA

· GOING OUTSIDE ·

CHICHAGOF ISLAND

N

Sitka

across the wilderness sky is the quintessential sound of Alaskan energy. And of all the planes working the bush, it is the De Havillands that hold a special niche.

The amphibious Otter stands ticking with heat on the weathered concrete runway of the Gustavus Airport. While its 600-horsepower Pratt & Whitney engine cools, the pilot skids the last of the Juneau load—backpacks, hard goods, and frozen food—out the portside cabin door and into the arms of the townspeople.

The De Havilland Otter, a big, high-winged float-plane, is the last of the radial engine bush planes, a Canadian design of the 1940s, built in the fifties, and still flying today. With its boxy fuselage, shiny propeller, bulbous engine cowling, visible rivets, and portholes for windows, the Otter would be a museum piece in the Lower 48. But her rugged airframe, a stall speed of fifty miles an hour, and a carrying capacity of roughly one-third her weight are precisely the characteristics needed in an airplane for the Alaskan bush.

It takes an Otter to carry several paddlers and their breakdown kayaks, provisions, and camping gear in one load to a remote water landing on the weather-beaten Alaska coast. We fit in the plane without much ado. The pilot, flying his first summer in Alaska territory, buckles up, and the massive radial engine shatters the conversations in the cabin. I quickly tear the preface page of my trip book into strips, sacrificing it for earplugs, as the plane thunders its way into a south wind and lifts into the air.

The Otter hangs just below a flat, grey ceiling at 1,000 feet on a westward bearing. We passengers, strangers for now, isolated from each other by the din, press our noses to the portholes, lost in reading the shoreline. Our introductions at the airport had been hurried. But there will be time to get acquainted, for we are soon to be sharing sea kayaks and paddling perhaps the most adventurous sea kayaking tour on the market, the ocean coast of Chichagof Island.

The pilot alters course to fly through North Inian

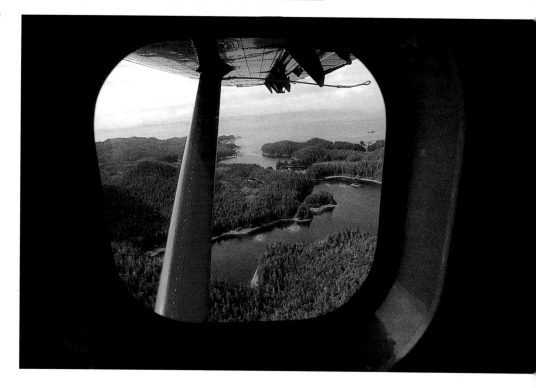

Pass, taking Cape Spencer to starboard, Yakobi and Chichagof islands to port. To those familiar with these parts, we are "going outside," leaving the famous route of the Alaskan gold prospectors—the protected water-way known as the Inside Passage—for the notorious waters of the Gulf of Alaska and the open Pacific.

The plane enters the cloud cover; we strain for last looks, and gaze across the cabin as rain streaks the windows. There are five of us—a physical therapist on contract in Anchorage, a New York photographer, a man who runs a gas station in Texas, our Gustavus-based guide, and I. We all appear to have the same thought: "Oh Lord, not nine days of rain."

We are bound for one of the largest islands of the Southeast Alaska archipelago. Chichagof, named in 1805 by Russian explorers, covers 2,500 square miles of wilderness big enough to claim its own mountain range.

Port, strut, and wing of the De Havilland Otter frame the leading edge of islands off Chichagof's west coast.

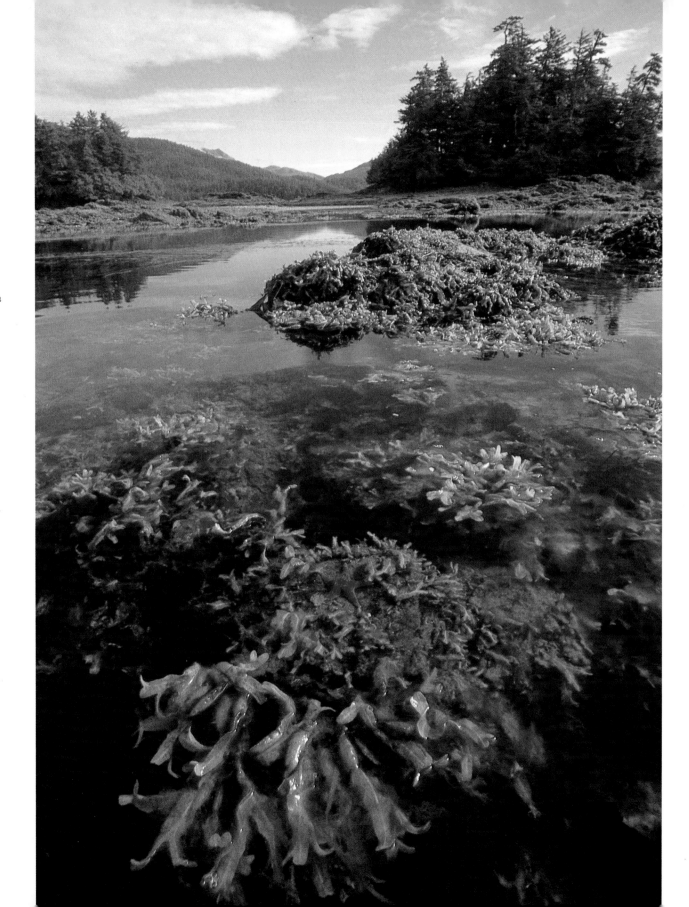

On a hot, low-tide
afternoon, fucus
frames a sea star in
the protected
lagoons inside
Dry Pass.

· GOING OUTSIDE ·

This island is a part of Alaska frequented only by salmon fishermen, winter deer hunters out from Juneau 100 miles to the east, and the odd prospector. Too rugged, too wet, too remote for people to stick, it has an unwritten history of a few Tlingit villages, eighteenth-century Russian sea otter hunters, beach loggers, and miners all long gone.

I can tell by the compass we've turned south. The pilot, unbeknownst to us, is searching for a way down through the clouds. It is an uneasy moment, flying blind. The cabin dims as we pierce the cloud centers. The rain increases suddenly, and just as suddenly drops away. A darker patch beneath us proves to be a gap in our cloud floor, revealing a shadowed sea, breaking surf on battered rock, a treed shore. The Otter banks steeply into a descending spiral. We passengers unused to such maneuvers white-knuckle it as we drop through the hole and into the clear.

We turn inland, the Otter descending, while the pilot scans a series of inlets that cut into the island's mountainous spine. He reads the chart and confers with our guide, and then banks the Otter once again and turns into the wind. We land with the elegant smoothness of a floatplane on flat water.

The huge propeller rotates to a stop and the Otter glides to a fine gravel beach, littered with expired salmon and enveloped in a ringing quiet. One by one, we hop from the floats to dry ground and take in the panorama. Toward the sea lies a low agglomeration of irregular islands softened by a full forest covering. Across the still water, salmon randomly leap at the low clouds and fall back with a substantial plop. At our backs, the spawning stream they seek falls through the trees, then meanders briefly through a high grass marsh to meet saltwater just down the beach.

The pilot and guide are already unpacking the plane. We form a chain and quickly unload our food, gear, supplies, and our precious kayaks. In the long, blue bags are the Nautiraids—French double kayaks made with a laminated wood framing and a rubberized fabric

skin. I unpack my single Feathercraft enclosed in its own backpack that looks more like a compact red futon. Within lurks the answer to a question breakdown kayak owners on a remote beach commonly ask themselves as the floatplane turns into the wind and effortlessly flies away: "Are all the parts here?"

The Feathercraft has thirty parts. Its frame is a truly ingenious linkage of color-coded aircraft aluminum tubing that would look and behave like a deflated blimp if one part were missing. I lay them out: bow keel, port and starboard chine and deck ribs, seat frame, and rudder. Piece by piece I fit tube to tube, color to color. Then I insert the bow frame into the very red fabric skin, followed by the stern frame. I lever the extension tubes to tightness and voilá—a sixteen-and-a-half-foot sea kayak, all parts fitted in fifteen minutes, ready for sea. I rest easy, the salmon jump, the rain stops. We load the group gear and our personal belongings, and gently carry the boats to tidewater.

Breakdown kayaks are remarkable craft—certainly the closest contemporary adaptation of the ancient Eskimo and Aleut sea kayaks. Like their predecessors, they bend and work through the waves. Though they usually carry less and are not quite as fast as their rigid fiberglass cousins, their versatility is unquestioned. They make this trip possible.

We paddle for two hours into the late afternoon, covering five miles of forested passes and still water in open, lakelike crossings before holing up on a small island, well back from the ocean. Nate Borson, our guide from Spirit Walker Expeditions, helps us unload the kayaks before we all hoist them above the tideline. A campsite is picked on one grassy end of the island, and our bear-attracting kitchen goes on the other.

As an unseen August sun lowers in the west, we settle in for an all-you-can-eat dinner of smoked salmon, a salad of fresh Gustavus vegetables, and home-baked bread. Between bites, our eyes survey our new world. It's definitely not Texas City, Texas, as Dan Reader ponders how he's going to get his new wool

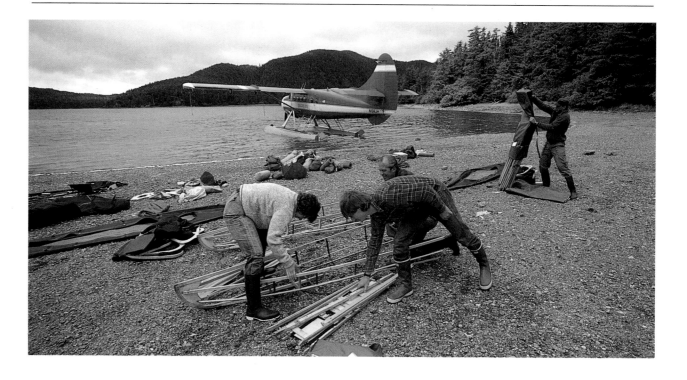

◆

The Otter prepares for its return to Gustavus, while parts and pieces of Nautiraids and Feathercrafts are spread across the beach by willing kayakers.

socks dry. To Alan Fortune, who was living and working in Manhattan forty-eight hours ago, it is a photographer's dream come true. And Tamara Beaulieu, just recently moved to Anchorage from Michigan, looks upon this seascape as her new backyard.

I am curious why these people signed on for a kayak trip to the wild and woolly ocean coast of Alaska when they have little or no experience in sea kayaks. Over some Red Zinger tea, I find the common thread is a strong desire to experience wilderness Alaska, intertwined with a love of water, ocean coasts, and a curiosity about sea kayaks. To Tamara, it's more than curiosity. A long-distance cyclist, she chose this trip not only to see a unique part of Alaska but to learn another way to move naturally through the world.

Nate loves that response. It is his job to teach the beginners paddling, steering, safety, and rescue techniques, as well as to shape us all into a responsible team

that cares for the environment, the equipment, and each other throughout the trip. I realize that our combined skills limit us to good-weather traveling and that we might get stormed in somewhere. If that happens, we'll just have to wait for the weather to clear and the Otter to come to our rescue. We talk into darkness this first night, listening to the periodic plop of the salmon, adjusting to being on our own, in good company, well away from anything familiar.

Morning brings a promise of improving weather. As I carry my belongings to my waiting kayak, I take in our setting with a new appreciation. The clouds have lifted, revealing a range of 2,000-foot peaks. One, Doolth Mountain, a curious name from the Tlingit meaning "everything good and plentiful," is shaped like a child's drawing. Standing alone, it rises up from the dark waters of the bay like an inverted sno-cone, cloaked in distinct zones of moss-green forests, grass-bright meadows, and a naked rock summit. A fault, like an ancient scar, creases its southern flank. I can see the tailings of old gold mines following the cleft up over the ridge, mute evidence of the played-out claims of the Alaska gold-mining days.

The low tide reveals our own golden tailing of rock-clinging fucus, that air-filled translucent yellow seaweed that pops when you step on it. Gingerly, we set the kayaks at the water's edge and load amidst the sounds of expiring fucus bladders. The cold sea water presses against my boots, as I gauge just how far from shore I can stand to load my kayak without getting wet. Everyone is busy, carefully packing dry bags into the bows and sterns of the double kayaks. Nate judiciously hands out the divided group gear to each of us. I take the stove, some fuel, and the lunch bag, and pack the food within easy reach.

We are anxious to get paddling, to get to sea. Nate lifts the bow of Dan and Tamara's double off the beach. I drift offshore and watch Nate as he oversees the new kayakers getting squared away—spray skirts fitted to coamings, rudders down, paddles right side up. I find myself wondering whether his is an enviable job.

Over the past decade, about fifty sea kayaking guide services have sprung up throughout the world. Founded by sea kayakers searching for a way to make a living doing what they love, today most of the principals paddle a computer while their hired guides work season-long, seventy-hour weeks, learning to deal with short-fused clients and lost kayaks and not making much more than $3,000 a summer. The true rewards are time spent kayaking, being with kindred spirits, the potential for romance one outfit calls "the retirement plan," and living life in the wilderness. As Nate settles into the rear seat of his Nautiraid, I am again struck by how similar he is to the many guides I've come to know. They are, both men and women, easygoing personalities, with rugged good looks, simple lifestyles, and a strong environmental consciousness. Money is not everything.

Vorota Island: *Vorota* means "the gate" in Russian.

It is a stopper island, nearly blocking the mouth of Klag Bay and the placid waters of our put-in. We paddle through the narrow channel like kids going outdoors to play, our world changing with every forward stroke. Before us lie a hundred islands festooned along the outer edge of Chichagof—geologically sharp-edged islands, islets, and reefs showing white as the wind-generated swells break against their granite margins.

Instantly, we are taking wind and chop from due north. I lean forward to zip up my sprayskirt and pull my McCall, Idaho, baseball cap on tighter. Instinctively I'm gripping my paddle shaft too tightly. I tell myself to ease up as I rudder right, bringing my bow back up on course. We're going to get wet. I look back and see Dan and Tamara fighting their first wind. Tamara, in the bow, takes a shot of spray, laughs, paddles, and laughs again. Dan is busy learning to hold the kayak on course; he lets the boat fall off broadside to the wind, forcing them to work harder to regain their course. In time, he begins to anticipate the waves and winds, as Nate shepherds us along the windward edge of the first islands.

This is not the open ocean; the thick sweep of islands and islets off our port bows blocks the sea swell. Instead we are crossing the southern entrance to Ogden Passage, a three-mile fetch of water, open to the wind that creates the waves we are experiencing—steep and short, averaging one to two feet—just right for the new paddlers to get their sea legs. I watch Dan in the stern now paddling in unison with Tamara in the bow, working as a team. Midway across, the wind increases to a steady fifteen miles per hour with gusts to twenty. Nate guides us into the lee of a convenient islet for a rest stop.

Tamara, Dan, and Alan are discovering how their boats behave; they know what happens if you let your paddle catch the wind. (Strong winds can knock a paddle out of an unwary kayaker's hand, even knock the paddler(s) off balance and cause a capsize.) And Nate now has a better idea of how his people will react in similar conditions. Recharged, we head out on a

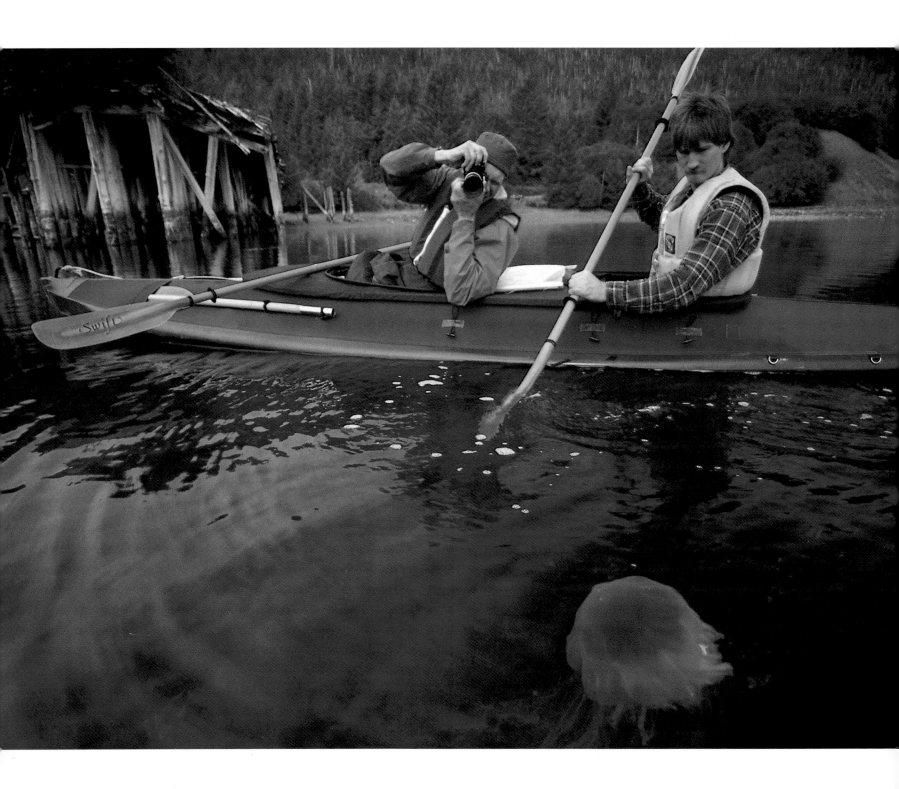

different course—paddling off the wind, taking the waves at a forty-five-degree angle. As we build a comfortable rhythm, we must be making close to four knots. Smiles cross faces as "glory holes"—blue-sky breaks in the cloud cover—appear.

By late afternoon we have threaded our way out of the wind, well into the Granite Islands, stopping just short of the open ocean. A white shell beach between two unnamed islets looks like home. We land and spread out to select tent sites, our stiff, soggy legs taking us into the forest of the larger northern islet and up a grassy slope. I find the remains of a sea lion, too far from shore to have gotten there on its own. But I see no sign of bears, just deer trails everywhere. I scout upwind, surrounded by the mottled grey trunks of coastal spruce, conscious of how few people have ever been here, conscious of the wind that once again threatens rain.

The Tlingit people of Chichagof believe the ravens are the official alarm clocks of all creatures. Two, perhaps three, ravens are calling now, in the half-light of dawn, well above the forest canopy. It is a call unlike anything I've ever heard: a melodious, metallic plonk like a raindrop striking a tin drum. From my sleeping bag I steal a glance out the tent—blue sky. Another look toward the distant kitchen down amongst the beach driftwood reveals life: Nate is making coffee and Alan stands atop the logs thinking about taking pictures. Plonk.

Today is magic. The sky stays blue and the sun warms us. Chichagof lies stretched out before us. Doolth Mountain is now but one of a series of peaks stretching from Sitka to Cross Sound. In the clear, smog-free air we can see sharp details of the 12,000-foot-high Fairweather Range emerging from the sea seventy-five miles in the distance.

We paddle on the rim of the Pacific, rising and falling in a world of liquid energy, riding the cobalt-blue backs of the great trans-Pacific swells. Our course runs parallel with the line of the waves that creates for us a world of peaks and valleys, our kayaks model ships in

hurricane-sized seas. We stay within shouting distance as we watch one another drop out of sight behind an endless succession of waves. They come in sequences—most are perhaps fifteen feet high, but occasionally some are larger, menacing, so big they seem steep enough to break on us. For a moment, I sit in the trough, staring at the building wall of water that has traveled thousands of miles, rolling down on me, effortlessly lifting my kayak to the sky, and then rolling away—living its final moments before crashing against the continent.

By afternoon we've reached the Myriad Islands, moving back into calm, shallow passes and utterly still bays. Mimicking the stealth of Tlingit hunters, with our cameras Alan and I stalk deer feeding along the tideline. We glide smoothly through the shallows; seastars and sculpins slide beneath our keels as we take care not to go aground. By four o'clock we are island-camped again, boats and bodies angled into the sun atop a pebble beach in seventy-degree weather.

Our window of blue sky lasts through the following day—long enough for us to weave a ten-mile trail through the Myriad Islands and into Ogden Passage and Portlock Harbor. But this is the Alaska panhandle, where measurable precipitation is a near-daily occurrence. By the evening of the fifth day it is raining, and we are a picturesque group huddled beneath a free-standing, blue-and-white-striped tarp, looking for the world like an outdoor wedding reception gone awry.

Our awning is big enough to shelter our kitchen and ourselves, but it is sited well below the high tide line. Nate explains: "Bears. There are very few campsites on the mainland of Chichagof—usually only on the outwash plains of the salmon streams. There's not only not enough flat ground there, but also there's a good possibility of a bear visit. As long as we keep our kitchen within the intertidal where the water can wash away any scent of our meals, we minimize the chance of local bears associating this campsite with food."

Left: Mesmerized, Alan and Nate watch the motions of a jellyfish near the ruins of a Doolth Mountain gold mine.

Wise strategy. In my travels, I have encountered three so-called "problem" bears that frequently raid favorite sea kayaker camps. In the Queen Charlotte Islands, there's "Benjie" of Benjamin Point. The Glacier Bay National Monument rangers have a constant problem with bears becoming too familiar with campers and kayakers. With enough incident reports on a particular bear, the rangers will helicopter the offending animal into a less peopled region. In an extreme case the bear is shot, as was the case on Prince William Sound's Culross Island after a "garbage bear" began stalking people. We ask the obvious question of Nate: "Have you ever had a bear confrontation?" And we are relieved to hear him say, "No, Spirit Walker has never had anything beyond sightings."

Still, it's strange dining amidst the fucus. We now time our meals with the tidal rhythm—eating when the tide is low, day tripping or sleeping ashore when the tide is high.

It has been tough to return to rain; our energy just sags. The next morning, Nate has to nudge us along to break camp. We roll and stuff wet tents, and agonize over the incredible creeping damp that claims one sock after another. But once snug in our rain gear and paddling warm, our enthusiasm returns. We travel beneath the cloud-draped summits, past an oriental rainscape of wind-sculpted forests, spongy muskeg, steep cliff faces, and waterfalls plummeting to deep bays.

When we get to Dry Pass, the rain lightens. Nate pulls us over at the last protected beach before the open ocean, to scout the sea conditions outside. The same swells we had ridden so happily in the sunshine a few days before are grey and ominous today. Dry Pass is a tight opening to the outside, something we wouldn't take in any rougher weather or lower tide. Nate is jubilant; with calm seas by Alaska standards, we are going to make White Sulphur Hot Springs.

Yes, hot springs. It's all we can do to set the boats high up on the logs before we're on the trail to 104-degree bliss. The Forest Service maintains the springs and an adjacent cabin. We experience mixed emotions when we arrive. Other people are there: two kayakers all the way from Ketchikan and four folks in from Juneau on a floatplane. Some of us get a little shy, but introductions are made as we slip our naked bodies into the faintly sulphur-smelling pool, and conversations begin. We stay until we are nicely poached.

Nate is on edge during our last evening meal because of the changeable weather. He listens again to the Sitka NOAA weather forecast and says nothing. We have to be back on the lagoon side of Dry Pass for our floatplane pickup the next day, retracing yesterday's four miles of open ocean and lee shore, not to mention reentering the pass. Should it begin to blow, we'd be in trouble. A good kayak guide, Nate presents an alternative: we can portage through the forest to Sea Level Slough, where the Otter can land and meet us. Repetitive trips backpacking our gear and kayaks a mile distant sounds like work to us. We instantly begin offering little prayers to our personal weather gods, and the night stays calm. Alan and Nate take one last dip in the hot springs, and we depart White Sulphur, paddling to an unexpected sun rising through sparse clouds.

Alan and I jockey our kayaks for position as we move out through the protecting islets off the hot springs bay. Once through Caution Pass, we enter a large semicircular bay bathed in the delicate light of early morning. The sea's surface is windless, swathed in golden white spindrift. I rudder outboard of the two Nautiraids and paddle hard for position, turn, and grab for my camera. Alan and Nate pass close by, and Tamara and Dan are in the background—all framed by the exquisite sea-to-mountain setting of Chichagof. I focus, frame, and shoot until I finish the roll, and drift to a stop. My cameras are weightless as I enjoy the pleasure of having taken one of my best photographs. I fit a new roll, set the cameras back in their dry bag, and race to catch up. In the distant sky, way to the east, I hear the unmistakable drone of a radial engine.

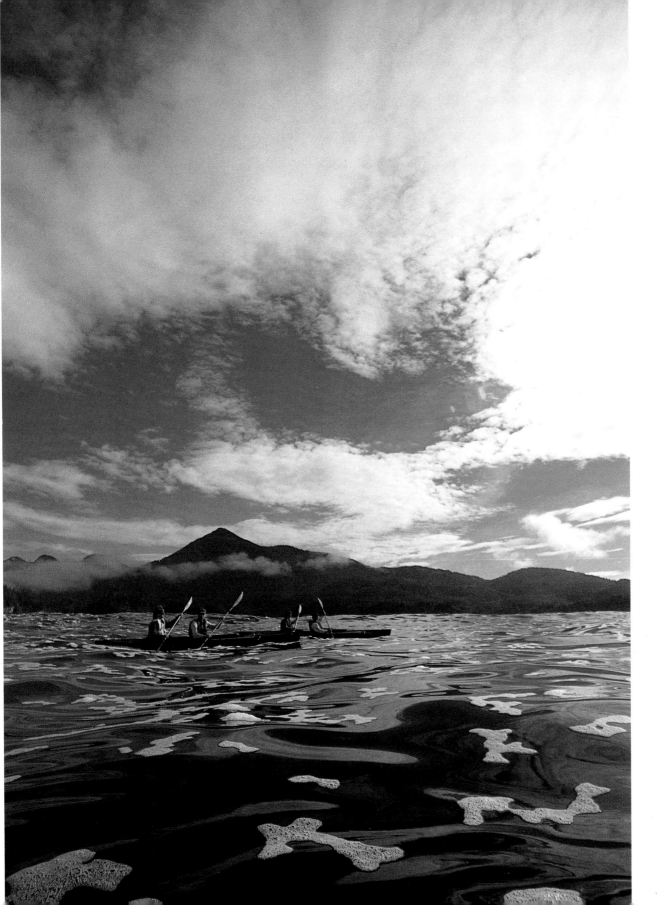

◆

The clarity of Alaska's light and the patterns of sea foam play to the photographer off White Sulphur Hot Springs.

THE KNIFE'S EDGE

◆

The Queen Charlotte Islands

IF YOU WERE to kayak from the cities of the Pacific Northwest coast, beyond the margins of the last towns, beachfront homes, and marinas until only the forest and the sea lay off your bow, you would be tracing a course of a people who long ago paddled these waters.

From the Gulf of Alaska to the southern end of Puget Sound, these coasts were once the world to the Tlingit, Tsimshian, Haida, Bella Bella, Bella Coola, Kwakiutl, Westcoast, and Coast Salish. These first inhabitants of the Northwest Coast, like the coastal Eskimo and the Aleut of Alaska, were a sea people who created a culture built around the utility of a boat. Hewn from the massive red and yellow cedars, the dugout canoe of the Northwest Coast natives was their vehicle for hunting whales, fishing, traveling, and waging war. It was their vehicle in myth and legend. And now its spirit returns in a new form, the modern

Left: Bear, thunderbird, and orca in carved cedar— Haida mortuary totems stand at Ninstints, imposing in decay.

Masset

G r a h a m
I s l a n d

BRITISH COLUMBIA

Hecate Strait

Queen Charlotte City ● ● Skidegate ● Sandspit

PACIFIC OCEAN

Moresby Camp ●

Cumshewa Inlet

Moresby Island ● Skedans

Lost Island

Lyell Island *Windy Bay*

Burnaby
Island

Dolomite Narrows

· THE KNIFE'S EDGE ·

THE QUEEN CHARLOTTE ISLANDS

● Rose Harbour

Kunghit
Island

Ninstints

N

kayak, as a vehicle, a guide, and a teacher for a new people to find the ways of the past.

Choosing to travel by your own strength and skill, you can meet some of the challenges of the native paddlers. Suddenly you share the same wet dimension, the same pace and rhythm of the day, a common awareness of weather and distance, the ability to explore intricate coasts, and the intimate knowledge all of that brings. As you make the daily decisions of whether to paddle, when to camp, and where the bottom fishing might be good, you begin to feel a kinship with the natives who once called these waters home.

In time, as you journey farther from civilization as we know it, you may see the faint signs of the old civilization, one that flourished for over 8,000 years, poking out of the forest and along the beach, arousing your curiosity about these people who are famous for their totem poles and magnificent longhouses. And then one day you may enter a protected bay, land on a white shell beach beneath an unusual grass berm, and realize that this is not only a good campsite, but an old village site. You become aware that the depressions in the ground are the remains of the great cedar longhouses, and the berm beneath your feet is a midden—an accumulation of cast-off shells from centuries of ancient feasts.

If you find yourself trying to visualize the original village, asking what it was like to live here, wanting somehow to go back in time, to know the people of the cedar canoes, then you are ready to make the journey to the Queen Charlotte Islands.

Remote and unfamiliar, swept by the Pacific, separated from the British Columbia coast by a treacherously shallow fifty- to eighty-mile-wide strait, the Queen Charlotte Islands are a misty kingdom of islands and mountains, giant spruce and cedar forests, peregrine falcons and Steller's sea lions. They are, for their wildness alone, a sea kayaker's dream.

The Charlottes are a Canadian Galápagos, having the largest percentage of endemic plants, birds, mammals, and insects found anywhere in North America. The islands shelter great seabird rookeries, and are home to the world's largest black bears and to eleven species of whales. But it is the more than 400 Haida archaeological sites that draw the kayaker to the Queen Charlottes, to paddle in the traces of the cedar canoes and wander through the deserted villages.

The Queen Charlottes' two major islands are distinctly different land forms: Graham to the north is relatively flat, with few offshore islands, and Moresby to the south is mountainous and hemmed with islands. Both islands' western coasts are victim to unpredictable and often violent Pacific storms. Because of these factors there is one favored route to kayak in the Charlottes—the southeast coast of Moresby Island.

Moresby is a 100-mile-long island ridged with 4,000-foot peaks that deflect and block the energy of the Pacific, sheltering the fjords and forested islands along its eastern shore. Few people live here; it is a true wilderness, and much of it has never been logged. The few mines have shut down, and the whaling station has rotted into its bay. The towns of the Charlottes—the Haida villages of Skidegate and Masset, the airport town called Sandspit, and Queen Charlotte City with its ferry route to the mainland—lie safely to the north. Only the loggers have threatened the nature of Moresby.

Over the past twenty years, a protracted battle to save the old-growth forests of Moresby has been waged by the Haida, local whites, and concerned environmentalists who blockaded operations to clearcut the island's entire forest. The world took notice, and the government of British Columbia grudgingly moved to establish the South Moresby National Park Reserve. In the end, the line was drawn at Lyell Island. To the north, thirty miles of Moresby's timber and most of Graham Island's trees will be clearcut. To the south for seventy miles, the 1,000-year-old cedars, Sitka spruce, and western hemlock are safe: there are 1,000 miles of wilderness seashore to paddle, with over 100 emerald islands to visit without any clearcuts from beach to summit.

In the early summer, I join Steve Jones and John

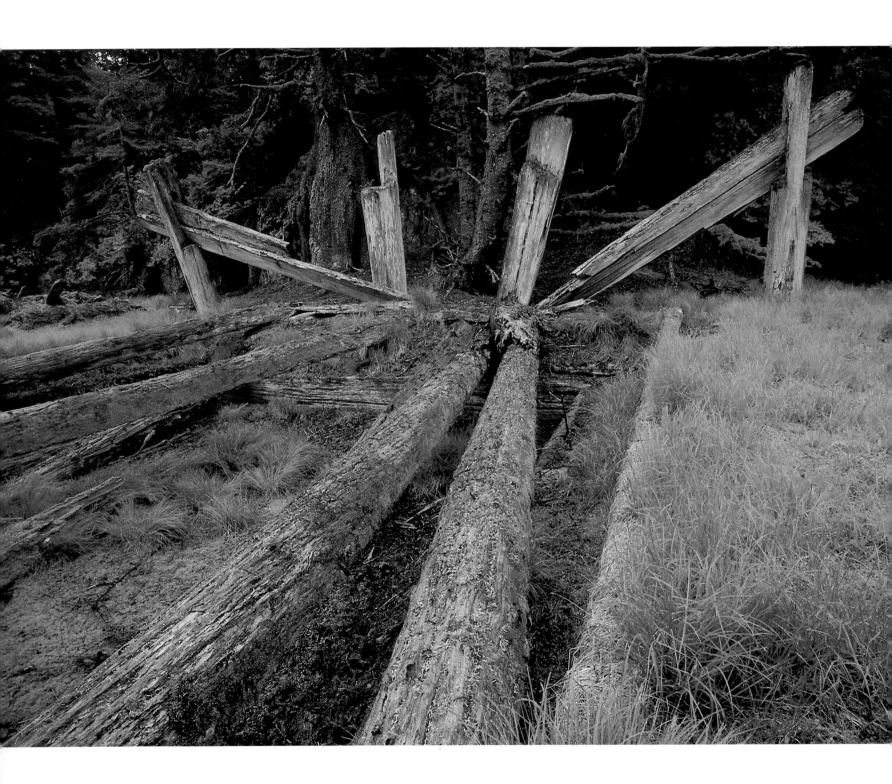

· THE KNIFE'S EDGE ·

Eddy for two weeks of paddling the eastern edge of South Moresby. We stash our cars at Port Hardy on the northern tip of Vancouver Island, and as on the Alaska ferry, we carry our kayaks aboard. After arriving at Queen Charlotte City, we charter a converted salmon troller for a lift to the southern end of South Moresby, and disembark at a place called Rose Harbour, two hours paddling distance from Ninstints, the last ancient native village site still standing on the west coast of the Queen Charlottes.

Ninstints is the first of four places we will visit that retain the soul of this misty kingdom. The others are Dolomite Narrows, Lost Island, and Skedans. Like Ninstints, they perhaps best illustrate what influenced the Kunghit Haida to call their Queen Charlottes *Gaawa Hanas*, the "Place of Wonder."

∿∿∿

Ninstints was a town of twenty longhouses and over 300 people when smallpox came. Over a decade, family by family, house by house, the people died, until Ninstints was abandoned in 1875. The survivors fled to Skidegate, where remnant populations of all the stricken southern villages struggled to understand, to live, and to maintain their culture. By the turn of the century, the Haida had been decimated to one-tenth their original population. Ninstints was left open to the wind and weather.

Beyond the water's edge, rising above the beach grass, framed by a backdrop of encroaching evergreens stands a line of thirty totem poles. They are at least 130 years old, their weathered, silver-cedar faces mute: Bear Mother, Killer Whale, Sea Grizzly, and Cormorant stare out to sea in broad, bold relief. These carved forms of both natural and supernatural creatures are symbols and signs of ownership, called crests, that represent the wealth and power of the family that lives in their shadow. The setting, the experience of paddling beneath their ageless stares, still convey that power.

◆

Far left: Roof stringers of solid cedar logs, twenty-five inches in diameter and forty-five feet in length, lie fallen across the central common room and family terraces of "House that is Always Shaking" at Ninstints.

Left: The skeleton of a purple sea urchin lies on the forest floor—the remains of a one-time meal carried far into the trees. Windy Bay, Lyell Island.

We too are silent.

I walk up onto a natural terrace and into an intricate web of ancestral memories, sacred sites, and complex myths beyond my imagination. I drift silently among the totems and walk the perimeter of the longhouse depressions. Cloudy House was home to the "Striped Town People." Mountain House sheltered "Those Born in the Southern Part of the Islands." And at the south end of the bayfront, the large forty-six-foot by forty-nine-foot Thunder-Rolls-upon-It House once stood, where the last chief, Ninstints, and his people, "Those Born up the Inlet," lived and died.

The Haida named everything—every house, reef, mountain, and rocky beach—not simply to assign a place-name but to integrate each entity into a belief structure that was passed from generation to generation. Often varying from family to family or village to village, their legends offered explanations for a world in which the sky at night sometimes blazed, the salmon swam to their feet, and men sometimes paddled from this cove never to be seen again.

George F. MacDonald, in his beautiful ethnography *Haida Monumental Art: Villages of the Queen Charlotte Islands*, described the world as perceived by the Haida:

> *To the Haida, their world was like the edge of a knife cutting between the depths of the sea, which to them symbolized the underworld, and the forested mountainside, which marked the transition to the upper world. Perhaps because of their precarious position, they embellished the narrow human zone of their villages with a profusion of boldly carved monuments and brightly painted emblems signifying their identity. Throughout their villages these representations of the creatures of the upper and lower worlds presented a balanced statement of the forces of the universe.*

The view from among the totems passes over our kayaks and out through the cove's entry. I realize that where I stand, listening to the wind and measuring the whitecaps across the channel, I've found the best vista from the terrace, the point where whether to go fishing must have been discussed from time immemorial. For a moment our kayaks become cedar dugout canoes, imaginary children run naked across the pebbles, there are songs from the row of longhouses mixed with the garrulous voices of ravens in the treetops. For a moment I'm there, in prehistory, in Ninstints.

A new urgency in the wind, backing to the southeast, brings me to the present. We cannot stay on the island; it is sacred to the Haida, maintained by them, and since 1983 watched over by a resident caretaker. We linger as long as we can and then slip quietly out of the bay late in the afternoon.

~~~

The day is fair and windless, deep in the protection of Moresby's mountains. The descending hillsides mirror themselves on the water of Dolomite Narrows, our bow-waves the only disturbance, our paddles making the only sound. Through the reflection of a clear blue sky, the bottom comes up to meet us. Wisps of kelly-green seaweed part to reveal mats of seastars, like an oriental carpet of rich colors—royal purples, coral reds, sky blues, and sea greens—all cruising about on thousands of tiny tube feet.

It is a bed of unexpected intensity, the sea life so concentrated, so plentiful, draped across the sea floor in what appears to be a backwater. But as we paddle farther in, the backwater becomes a tight pass 300 yards long, separating South Moresby from Burnaby Island to the east. Through it, the daily ebb and flow of phytoplankton-rich sea water squeezes north then south and back again, the current supporting the filter feeders. The entire intertidal is layer upon layer of expired butter clams. Over all, rock and spider crabs, turban snails, and starfish scuttle, fully conscious of our presence. Grounding ashore, I set my boots down between starfish, and the abandoned shells crumble with my weight.

Beyond the tideline, a deer grazes along a grassy bench that was once Narrow Strait village, one of three known settlements within an arrow's flight of the passage. Like many of the old village sites, Narrow Strait village has a parklike lawn between the sea and the forest. Deer, introduced to the island in the 1920s, gravitated to these open spaces created by village sites

◆

Right: Everywhere there are the subtle movements of small fish and crabs, and more subtle still the creep of snails and starfish for those patient enough to spend an afternoon drifting through Dolomite Narrows.

and have pruned any sapling that dared break ground ever since. We set up camp on the grass as the tide ebbs. The pass empties like the biblical Red Sea, the sunset highlighting random arcs of clam squirts.

~~~

Why is it that so many epics begin with "we got a late start"? It must have been 10:00 A.M. when we left camp, a small unnamed village site just east of Dodge Point on Lyell Island. John and Steve take an inside route, bound for the well-preserved longhouse foundations of Tanu village. I am captivated by the low silhouette of Lost Island, the most isolated island of the Charlottes, four and a half miles into Hecate Strait. We part company, planning to meet two days hence.

The weather is questionable, whitecaps are visible off the point, and the sky beyond is a sullen grey. As I clear the headland, doubt begins to creep in with the spray. Xe-u', the southeast wind spirit, is bringing rainy, tempestuous weather. Two miles out, I find myself in a steady twenty knots with four- to five-foot following seas about fifty feet apart. I'm soaked but warm enough and feeling strong; with each stroke my kayak strides across the grey seascape. Through a rain shower, I can barely see the island.

From beneath my hood I scan my surroundings, gaining a collective picture of wind, waves, greys, and greens in motion. A seabird is working upwind in my direction, using the shelter of the swell, disappearing in the trough, then rising and dumping wind at the crests. I watch with increasing fascination as it struggles toward me. When the bird is about thirty feet away, I realize it is a common murre bent with the wind, barely making headway. It does not see me. We drop into the same trough. Twenty feet, ten feet, right to my bow—wings flare in alarm. A tiny astonished eye holds mine for an instant, and we part abruptly.

I'm dazzled by the fact that we almost collided. A wave comes aboard, startling me, bringing me back to the wet present. I stroke hard to come back on course. The murre didn't see me because the wind is getting stronger, and the seas are building. I start to watch the wave train running up my starboard stern quarter. The significant waves, the one or two largest of a set of seven to ten waves known as a train, are now five to seven feet high and breaking. I turn to meet them, my paddle knifing their backsides.

I have been out no more than forty minutes when I turn and go with the train toward the shelter of Lost Island. Each wave builds behind me, raising my stern, almost sending my kayak rushing forward if it were not for my quick, chopping back-paddles to check the boat from surfing. Wave by wave, I approach the south side of the island—a windblown set of sea stacks with small forests in its cracks and draws. I recall that the chart showed a small cove that now becomes visible ahead. I pass the outer reefs, curl right, and paddle into flat, protected water.

I let out a triumphant yell: AaaaaaaaROOOOH. Two startled bald eagles guarding their nest natter at my announced arrival. Steller's sea lions on the inner rocks not more than forty feet off my bow don't show any interest in budging. I turn right toward a boulder beach, certain the sea lions haven't seen anyone here in years. They watch as I get out and stand, and then they bolt for the protection of the deep. They know man after all.

I turn toward higher ground, searching for a campsite, my mind on getting dry and making hot soup. I am relaxed and elated. Beneath the low, prickly needles of a spruce is a clearing strewn with flotsam—space for a tent and shelter for my stove. The wind howls beyond the bay. I look out at my boat with affection and the growing awareness that I'd been very lucky.

~~~

Like many of the villages, Skedans is on a tombolo—a spit connecting a small island to a larger landmass with bays on either side. Skedans has a fine

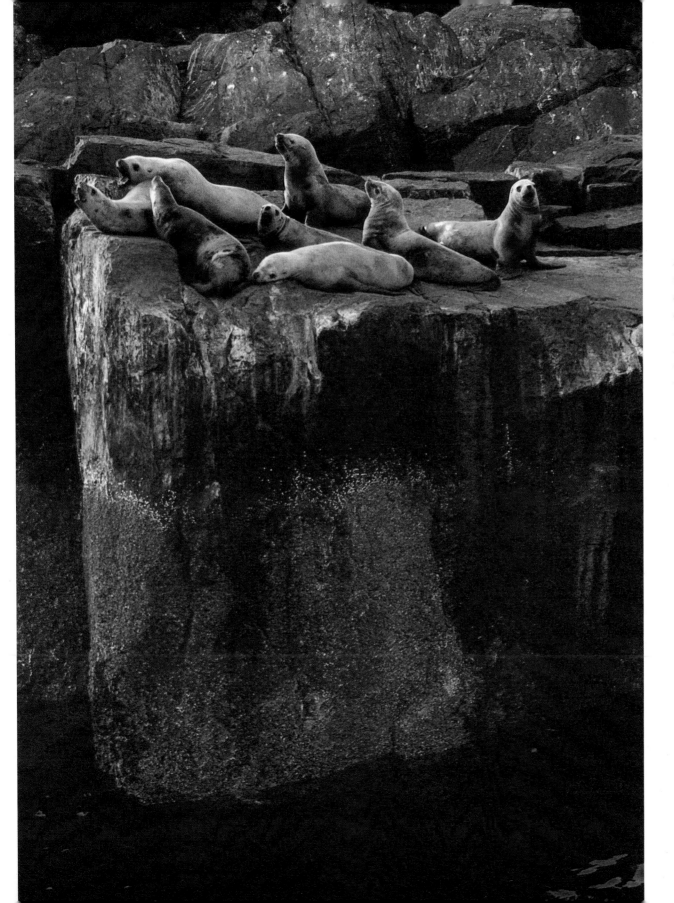

Steller's sea lions, their populations dwindling, are safe at home at Skedans Rocks, part of Environment Canada's marine reserve system.

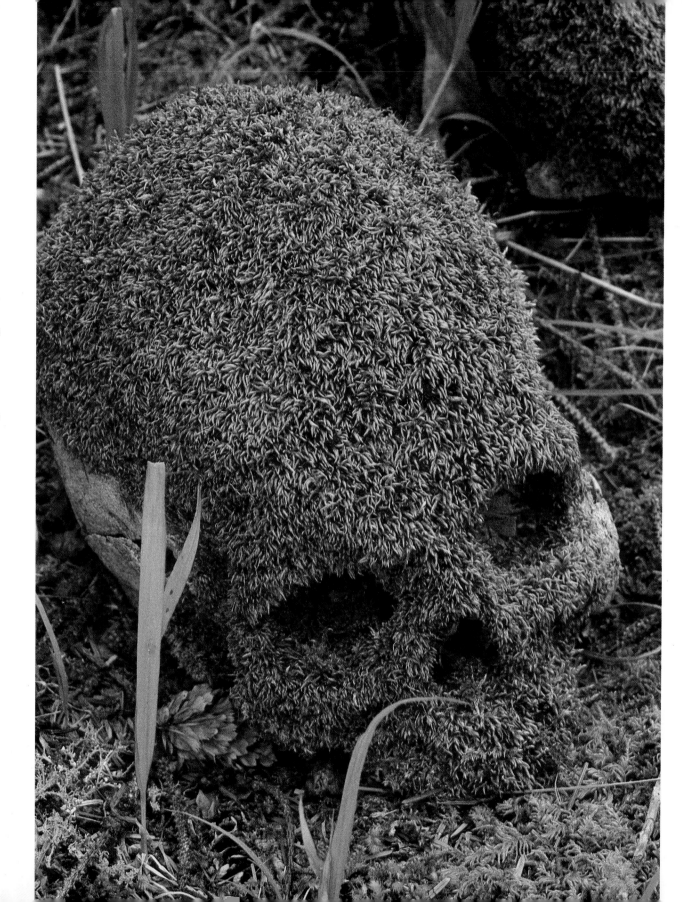

Time in reso-
nance—a grass
blade snipped by a
feeding deer, a
human skull fallen
from its mortuary
totem and covered
by a filigree of
moss—past and
present together at
Skedans village.

bay opening to the south. The twenty-six longhouses that once covered the spit faced the bay above a pebble beach. All that remains of them today are the depressions marking the individual house pits. Fifteen totem poles stand, lean, or lie throughout the village. Nearly all are mortuary poles—the legacy of sudden disease and the world's museums' preference for taking the taller and more elaborate house frontal poles.

Mortuary totems, about fifteen to twenty feet high, are carved with symbols that speak of the transition between worlds. In a cavity at the top were placed the remains of the house chief, and a painted front plaque acted as an epitaph. Near the center of the village is one such mortuary pole that has fallen toward the bay. Beside it, lying on the forest floor, is a skull sweatered with a delicate green moss. At first, approaching it from behind, I think it is a rounded rock. Then I see the eye sockets, the unmistakable shape of a human head. I stare at that skull, bone from a man that lived here over a hundred years ago, bone now so beautifully taken in by the nature of decay, as if being kept warm. Not without reverence, I take a picture and move away.

Still seeking spirits, I climb a promontory overlooking the village, again a vista for many ancient eyes, to sit and read, take some notes, and soak up some sun. A small black bear, perhaps a yearling, breaks from the forest at the far end of the bay, an intense blackness ambling along the beach. During my climb, I had come across the remains of a deer carcass and the depression left by a much larger bear who had fed continuously on the meat, leaving its scat in seven neat piles in a radial arc. I'm definitely going to hang the food bag at this campsite.

I watch the young bear nosing for food through the tideline piles of matted kelp. It will not see or smell me, and I am in no hurry to gain the beach. We go on about our separate interests until the noise of a Zodiac rounding the tombolo startles both of us. The bear hightails it and I step back into the cover of the forest, noting that we both had the same reaction to the arrival of people.

A party of seven, a non-native guide and six tourists, lands and fans out to explore.

I have not seen my partners for two days, and we had not seen anyone else since Rose Harbor; in time I work my way down the slope and into the village to say howdy. I encounter a scene of quiet embarrassment. One of the tourists has been caught secreting the skull in her knapsack, a memento of her trip to the Queen Charlottes. The guide is ashen; he has carefully replaced the skull in its bed of duff, and says to me if that skull had been stolen, the Haida tribal council might revoke his right to bring tourists to the villages. I'm troubled by the woman's indignation at being refused her "trophy." I mention the bear, and the group edges toward the Zodiac and away.

～～

Steve and John paddle into Skedans not much later, and we camp away from the village for the night. Our final day, an eighteen-mile slog into a grey, wet, moderate wind, takes us from Skedans up Cumshewa Inlet. With each stroke of the paddle, we are bringing to a close a trip into the prehistory of our coast that will haunt us for a lifetime. For the past fifteen days we have lived in the eddies of a culture so remarkable, it lives on in spirit not just throughout the glades of the abandoned villages, but in the reemerging culture of the Haida and within us as well.

The inlet is heavily logged and enclosed. At its head lies Moresby Camp, once a major booming yard, now home to a few homesteaders. The landing is littered with logging machinery and choker cable rusting in the rain, adding little to the bittersweet end of our trip. We are to be met by a man from Sandspit with a trailer for the boats and a case of "high-test" beer. But we aren't quite sure what day it is. Our man is nowhere to be seen. We stand around looking at our watches, momentarily captive to both the spirits of the land and the timetables from another world.

ORCA

♦

Johnstone Strait to Blackfish Sound

THEY COME OUT of the North Pacific depths in a coordinated attack. Orcas, the killer whales, quietly encircle the sockeye returning to the rivers of British Columbia. The salmon mill in confusion as the orcas, one by one, charge the center of the school. Those salmon prudent enough to flee discover the ring of orcas, like a net holding them in, each predator patiently awaiting its turn to feed.

It is early summer off the northwestern tip of Vancouver Island. The scent of the Fraser, western Canada's largest river, draws the salmon on as they follow their spawning urge, seeking their ancestral stream. They gather and turn south into the increasingly confining waters of Queen Charlotte Strait. The orcas follow, feeding at will.

By June, families, or pods, of orcas begin arriving at their summer "village." This gathering site is at the western entrance to a great passage of saltwater that continually floods and ebbs between the massive northern flank of Vancouver Island and the myriad islets and inlets that buffer the mainland of British Columbia. Known as Johnstone Strait, this entrance is one to three miles wide, forty-seven miles long, and over 1,000 feet deep. It is a natural gauntlet the salmon must run to find

Left: *Orcas eye-to-eye. While feeding, the whales of A-12 subpod surface and resurface among kayakers in Blackfish Sound.*

53

Queen Charlotte Strait

Swanson
Island

Blackfish Sound

Weynton Passage

Blackney Pass

Hanson Island

Harbledown Island

• Telegraph Cove

JOHNSTONE STRAIT

West Cracroft
Island

Vancouver Island

BRITISH COLUMBIA

· ORCA ·

JOHNSTONE STRAIT TO
BLACKFISH SOUND

Robson Bight

N

Tsitika River

their spawning grounds. During the five months the salmon pass this way, up to 170 blackfish, as orcas are also known, will congregate in these waters, herding salmon, teaching their children, families reuniting with families.

So too in June the humans come, heading north from the universities and research centers, passing through Seattle and Vancouver up the fabled Inside Passage to Johnstone. They bring with them underwater microphones, cameras, and computers. They bring, as well, a curious reverence for the orca that separates them from their brethren. For they have a common conviction that the orcas are something greater than one more precious organism swimming in the sea. They study the behavior of a marine mammal that rules the world's oceans and has captured the hearts of all who study it. Paul Spong, who initially approached studying the orcas as you would a laboratory rat, described in 1974 after six years of research a far different understanding:

[The orca is] an incredibly powerful and capable creature, exquisitely self-controlled and aware of the world around it, a being possessed of a zest for life and a healthy sense of humor, and moreover, a remarkable fondness for and an interest in humans.

This viewpoint was not easily accepted. The orcas had long been named killer whales—toothed whales that have no enemies and, in Dr. Spong's estimation, no fear. They have been witnessed by seafarers to be swift and effective hunters of all major fish and mammal stocks. The orcas themselves were hunted sporadically by the Japanese and the Norwegians, and shot at by every self-righteous fisherman out for the same catch. They were assumed to be ruthless, voracious killers. The assumption was wrong.

Into the 1970s, in both Canada and the United States, researchers' fascination with orcas and other whales resulted in a groping realization of these marine

mammals' remarkable abilities. The first studies were with captive dolphins, porpoises, and, beginning in 1969, orcas, often in the circus atmosphere of the new marinelands. The first tests were simple nose-the-proper-button-and-receive-half-a-herring physiological studies. But in Paul Spong's visual acuity research, something went marvelously wrong: after 2,400 half-herrings and a ninety-percent success rate, Skana, the first captive orca to be studied, began giving the incorrect answer time after time—her only way to tell the researcher, "I want a new game."

Skana continued the education of Paul Spong, at one time seeming to correct him for leaving off a pectoral fin on her portrait by pointedly wheeling about her pool, the omitted fin splashing the artist. On another, Skana slashed her teeth across Paul's bare feet, only touching and causing no pain. He recoiled in

Glistening shiny black, a young male orca stretches his dorsal fin to the sky over Blackfish Sound.

Log-boom chains
rust on the shore at
Telegraph Cove. It
is morning and the
forecast promises
good weather:
clouds but no rain,
fifty-five degrees
Fahrenheit, with
winds from the
north at five knots.

instinctive fright but returned his foot to the original position. Skana repeated the movement, her head rising out of the quiet pool, her teeth sweeping over his extended toes. Again Paul flinched, but being a dedicated experimental psychologist, he repeatedly dangled his foot. Each time, Skana would lunge until he controlled his involuntary reaction. Skana then stopped and vocalized, staring back at Paul from the middle of the pool. He then realized that she was intentionally deconditioning his fear of her, establishing a bond of trust.

Through the 1970s, the studies of orcas evolved. No one doubted the whales' intelligence; their gentleness and family loyalty turned public opinion into a love affair, yet no one really knew the orca. Dr. Spong began studying free as opposed to captive orcas in 1974, by establishing a research station on uninhabited Hanson Island at the northern entrance to Johnstone Strait. Taping their voices and monitoring their daily patterns in the tidal wilderness, Paul's research turned personal and public. Together with a growing family of researchers, film teams, writers, and musicians, the clinician became an advocate and a voice for the orca, and Johnstone Strait rippled to the wakes of kayakers, researchers, and orcas interacting in open curiosity.

In 1981, David Arcese had caught wind of Dr. Spong's studies and asked me to join him on a kayak trip to Johnstone Strait. Quiet, soft-spoken, fascinated by whales, David's curiosity about orcas must have rivaled Spong's. We were well into September, late for seeing orcas, but going anyway, as we car-topped our kayaks along Highway One north through the clearcuts and gentle peaks of interior Vancouver Island.

Our put-in was Telegraph Cove, a tiny, protected bay rimmed by second-growth evergreens. Along the back bayshore lay an exhausted timber mill whose saws had been stilled for a decade, a general store and a boat launch for the new economy of sport fishing, and a boardwalk connecting an unplanned string of sturdy fir-framed houses. With one green exception, these houses were painted white, roofed with corrugated tin, and each was well kept and lived in. They were sited along the tideline wedged between outcrops of granite and the stumps of long-gone old growth. Spartan, clean, dotted with the passing of ravens, Telegraph Cove was as it once was, hedged in by the landform, overlooked, blessed to grow no bigger.

We paid the store owner a small sum for launching privileges, and paddled out into Johnstone and a rising southeasterly. Hoping to be with orcas and intent on making Robson Bight eleven miles distant, we headed east hugging the Vancouver Island shore, our paddles feathered to knife the wind.

This first paddle to Robson would be a stormy one. Much of our time was spent grounded beneath a rain tarp, as a strong southeasterly tore up the strait. We saw only two orcas pass on our third day. The following morning, wet and cold, we packed and paddled back to Telegraph Cove, promising to return.

~~

Robson Bight is not quite a bay—it is a bend in the shoreline, an indentation deep enough to warrant a name but too exposed to give a vessel safe anchorage. In the years following our paddle to Robson, the bight would gain the attention of the world for its unique orca visitations. It would also narrowly miss becoming a timber booming yard, where the great log rafts would be created and towed to market. And its uplands, the climax forests of the Tsitika River valley—the last virgin watershed on the 285-mile-long island—would be slated for clearcutting. The government of British Columbia would designate the bight a marine ecological preserve in 1982, but in the end the timber industries have been allowed to cut the valley and only a 200-foot coastal buffer has been saved.

There were other changes: new paths and new attitudes were bringing new people to the water's edge. Each year another massive ocean liner joined the popular cruise ships sailing the Inside Passage. Two or three

ships a day passed the bight, immersing thousands of tourists into the magic of the forested islands, the eagles overhead, and, if they were lucky, the orcas. Telegraph Cove's old tug *Gikumi* had been converted to an orca-watching vessel, breathing new life into the Telegraph Cove economy. But one phenomenon stands out in the decade of growing interest over the orcas of Johnstone Strait: sea kayakers. These were newcomers with a relatively gentle impact, silently tracking to Robson Bight.

On a Sunday in July 1989, I returned to Johnstone Strait to meet up with David, who had founded Northern Lights Expeditions and was beginning his seventh season guiding sea kayakers into the strait. Amidst the salmon fishermen and whale watchers, we load and launch our group of twelve new kayakers into the little-changed harbor of Telegraph Cove. The weather is overcast and dry as we paddle out through the port entrance, the new seafarers bumping gunwales, hurtling this way and that as they learn to steer the fast, stable double kayaks. David and his assistant guide, Steffie Ackroyd, are moving like sheepdogs through the little flock, instructing and reassuring the neophyte kayakers, as we enter the open waters of Johnstone Strait.

As each pair of paddlers gets a rhythm going, we begin to speed up, relax, and take in our surroundings. Behind us hills of conifers rise up into the low clouds, hiding the steep 3,000-foot almost-mountains that crowd the northern shore of Vancouver. Before us, two miles of open water sweep away to the east and west to form the strait. Beyond the crossing lies Paul Spong's Hanson Island, one of a hundred low-lying islands to explore.

With the chart and a firsthand look at this landscape, I can realize, almost see, the forces that have shaped the scene before us. Off our bows, miles inland, the islands turn to mainland and rise to mountains, like a mirror image of Vancouver Island. Between these two natural barriers a millennium of glaciers has come and gone, rounding the islands' edges, mining channels as deep as 1,500 feet along the strait.

As we approach Hanson Island, David steers us toward Weynton Passage and the entrance to Blackfish Sound. We cheat as only a kayaker can, and paddle behind the tiny islets that rim the west end of the island, avoiding the main channel and the beginning of the opposing flood tide surging in from the Pacific.

Once through the pass, we stretch out into the open waters of Blackfish Sound, moving at a beginner's pace. This is a casual exploration; all of us are watching for orcas, some more impatient than others. David is in no hurry. After all his summers running trips along the strait, he knows the people in his charge will settle into enjoying all there is to see and do here—and see orcas.

David is good at this business, in part because he respects the spirit of the land as well as the orcas. He knows the locals and works with the Kwakiutl people of the region to protect their heritage sites. He is respected by the long-term researchers who help him set self-imposed guidelines on kayaking in the presence of whales. And he knows the orcas from his reading, attending conferences, and simply being here in contact.

In a few days, we'll move back across Johnstone to the camps north of Robson Bight where whale sightings are routine. For now, we get to know our kayaks and our partners as we paddle our way to camp.

We beach on a small pocket bay that faces south and set to unloading the boats and putting up tents. I wander through the kitchen and discover it is possible to snitch a fresh piece of cornbread. As our dinner of fresh salad and grilled cod, salmon, and crab disappears, we idly watch the evening go by. On the far side of our vista, the last of the salmon fishermen power back to Telegraph, the whine of their outboards fading toward the setting sun. A bald eagle soars off to the left, over a perfect little island. For many of the people on this expedition, this is their first day in company with eagles. Conversation stills as we watch the great scavenger wheel away.

◆

Left: Sheltered from the wind and anchored by kelp, a kayaker stretches in the sun after a visit to Robson Bight.

The mainland side of Johnstone Strait becomes a maze of narrow passes. The tide will transport you deep into a myriad of islands and six hours later flush you back out with memories of village sites, kingfishers, and a hermit's offering of fresh fish.

One of our group asks David about the small minke whale we'd seen earlier in the afternoon, when suddenly the ground begins to vibrate, strongly enough to stop the conversation. An ocean liner, massive and at speed, enters Blackney Pass southbound, passing our camp about a half-mile out. The light shines from the ship's cabins with the color of a campfire. I can almost imagine the disco music over the sound of the engines. Although we're close enough to see people, the decks are empty. The ship swings to ride the centerline of the 1,000-yard channel, comes around to port, steadies up on a course down Johnstone, and is gone. We stay quiet for a bit, to ruminate over this remarkable visitor. Elegant to some, an extravagance to others? No one says. We are undeniably on a different cruise.

The following days we explore Blackfish Sound, trailed by shy yet curious seals. Our real intent shows in our scanning of the way ahead for telltale dorsal fins, our ears tuned to the distant "whoosh" of orca breath. On the morning of our fourth day, we move our camp five and a half miles to the Vancouver Island side of Johnstone Strait for some serious orca watching. No sooner have we established camp than David spots a pod well out in the channel. We assist each other with our boats, and one by one we paddle from shore to intercept.

Whale watching is not unlike the behavior of a professional sports photographer on the sidelines of a football game. With every play, he moves farther down-field in an attempt to predict the advance of the team. The key to this analogy is that he cannot enter the field. Neither can we. Placing boats across the oncoming path of an orca pod might disrupt their activity—feeding, sleeping, playing—causing an unknown amount of stress to an already too popular mammal.

We paddle fast and hard, angling to approach the whales' course well ahead of them. David calls a halt and we gather into a group, staying still and hoping for the best. We wait. David had said that orcas have a distinctive cruising pattern of deep diving for three or four minutes at a time, then a series of shallow dives of ten to fifteen seconds duration. If we're in the right place, the pod should begin a shallow diving sequence about 200 yards off our bows. We wait and watch, necks swiveling left-right-left, fingers focusing lenses from thirty feet to infinity and back.

"They're behind us!" someone shouts, as the sudden sound of exhaling air reaches us across the water. We turn to face the pod. The whales surface again, and we do a sort of sotto-voce mutual squeal because they have turned, coming straight at us. At 100 yards, the orcas dive again and we go quiet, darting glances at each other. David says, "Just stay put."

One by one, their dorsal fins rise into the air right in front of us—so close it looks like a sure collision. At less than thirty feet, the largest bull aims right for me. I know from my reading and David's assurances that orcas do not intentionally attack or even bump kayakers in such a nonthreatening situation. I'm just trying to focus my camera. They dive, the male's six-foot dorsal fin sinking with a subtle side-to-side movement and I realize it's flexible, not knifelike, not a weapon. I look into the depths of mid-channel for the passing of the twenty-five-foot-long submarine shape, its dorsal fin faint in the watery darkness—five tons of *Orcinus orca* beneath my fifty-five-pound kayak.

We watch transfixed as the pod swims beneath us, their white-to-grey "saddles" across their backs marking their progress. The orcas make one final surface, each exhaling followed by a sharp intake of air, and they deep dive, tails rising from the water with an unhurried, fluid motion.

The water surrounding our kayaks ripples from sudden displacement. No one lifts a paddle. David suggests a course we can follow and we begin to move north toward Weynton Passage, keeping to the right of the pod's probable path.

In David's opinion, this pod is asleep. "Orcas sleep on the move, the adults taking turns on watch. See how they all breathe in unison." The pod surfaces well to our right, in easy rhythm, exhaling in the same uncanny synchronism; their high, jet-black dorsal fins rise and fall, parting the clear, jade-green water in mid-nap.

We learn that these four whales are called the C-5 subpod, a part of C pod, one of the larger resident families that summer in Johnstone Strait. The leader is C-5, the matriarch, the fifty-eight-year-old mother of C-2, a big dorsal-finned thirty-two-year-old male; C-10, an eighteen-year-old female; and C-13, a five-year-old toddler with the characteristic hook-shaped baby fin. These whales will stay together for life, a life that nearly matches ours in longevity.

Their colorless titles are disturbing—we would name them differently. David tells us that the numeric designations are a necessity for scientists. Whales in early studies were identified by more distinctive monikers—Wavy, Saddle, Nicola—with each name identifying a particular physical feature of the individual whale. But that became unworkable with the discovery of so many more whales at Johnstone.

Our own "pod" of fourteen kayakers looks pretty professional, paddling easily. Mirrored in the reflective greens and greys of the strait, our paddles rise and fall in unison, bow and stern sailors intent on the whales. Though David rarely shows it, he is pleased with the trip. We have achieved the skills to safely travel these waters, the people have warmed to the land's character, we all have been doing our dishes, and now we are in the company of orcas.

Suddenly the orcas' cruising pattern changes. They have doubled their speed, coming farther out of the water, awake and excited. The orcas have picked up echolocations from H pod, infrequent visitors to this area, moving through Weynton Passage and headed our way.

We paddle hard to keep up, but fall far behind as the giant mammals surge up the strait to greet their friends. The first orca breeches, his full body leaving the water, a 10,000-pound silhouette on the horizon, then a mammoth splash. Other orcas are "spyhopping" or swimming in place, propelling their upper torso clear of

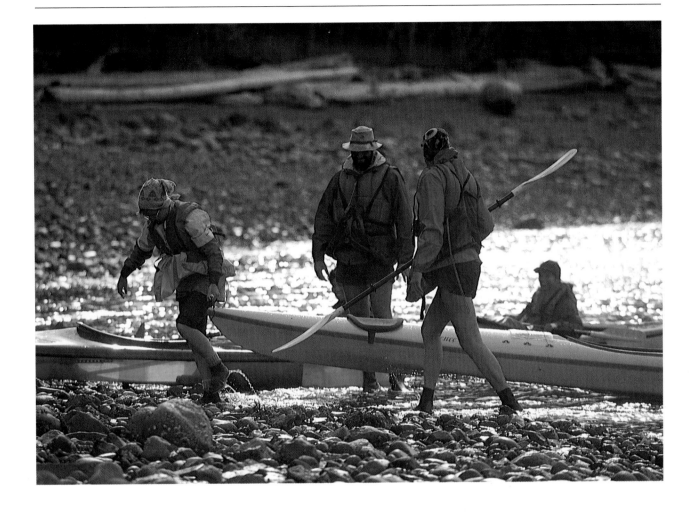

*At day's end,
kayaks are carried
high above the tide
line and the occa-
sional ocean
liner's wake.*

the water to see around them. Still others below are most likely curling around neighbors in physical touch. The sounds they are no doubt making underwater—clicks, whistles, and screeches—are identifications and greetings. Another whale breeches, this time close enough for us to see the distinctive markings of the whale's white and black stomach.

David brings us to a halt well short of the melee, at a 200-yard distance, grouped, watching. Gradually the hubbub dies, and we lower our cameras. The pods deep dive, showing their tail flukes, and minutes later they surface separated. The H pod continues with the tide along the east side of the strait, and C-5 subpod crosses back toward our camp.

We have had our close encounter. In the gathering dusk, C-5 and her family swim away, and we slow to a stop to watch them go. Clustered together, our paddles resting across our neighbors' boats, we try to verbalize the sensation of paddling with orcas, David every bit as animated as the rest. But words are insufficient. One by one, our paddles bite the still waters of Johnstone Strait for the Vancouver shore.

POINT OF CONTACT

◆

Nootka Sound

EIGHT A.M. Gold River, Muchalat Inlet, the west coast of Vancouver Island. The *Uchuck III* lists as her crew hoists a one-ton truck from the town pier into her forward hold. Surrounding the ship's hatch lie pallets of groceries, coiled wire, and tool boxes bound for the logging camps out near the coast. Alongside, boom boats shove and bump log rafts toward a shoreside paper mill. The air is fragrant with wood smoke, the fjord hazy in the morning sun.

The mate gestures for us to begin loading our six kayaks on the main deck, aft of the hold. My Polaris slides in behind Ross Anderson's old Escape on the sunny starboard side. The engines below rumble into life and go slow-astern. The *Uchuck* works on her springline and then comes ahead, entering the inlet, bound for Nootka Sound.

The ship gathers way on a westerly course, tiny in the immense geography of the inlet. Muchalat is fourteen miles long and less than a mile wide, bounded by 3,000-foot-high forest walls plunging another 1,500 feet

Left: Along the south side of Nootka Sound's Bligh Island is a small, magic beach where the sand stretches out beneath clear water to suspend kayaks as if in mid-air.

Boston Point

Bligh Island

Nootka Island

Cook Channel

Clerke Peninsula

Saltwater Lagoon

Friendly Cove

Yuquot

San Rafael Point

Nootka Sound

PACIFIC OCEAN

Vancouver Island

BRITISH COLUMBIA

Maquinna Point

Burdwood Point

N

· POINT OF CONTACT ·

NOOTKA SOUND

Aboard the
Uchuck III, Mary
Rothschild smiles
with apprehension
before the winches
lift her over
the side into
Nootka Sound.

to its silted fjord floor. Midway down the arm the sun has gained the ridge, and we bring full cups of coffee up to the stern rail. Shoulder to shoulder, we watch the *Uchuck*'s brilliant white wake pearl away, subsiding to racing blue-velvet waves that widen toward the dark-green hillsides.

The *Uchuck III*, a ship with the ironic Westcoast native name meaning "calm waters," is one of the last remaining coastal freighters on the West Coast. Once a World War II mine sweeper, the 136-foot-long, twenty-four-and-a-half-foot-wide, fir-hulled ship cuts a living out of the inlets and fjords of western Vancouver Island,

supplying the loggers and fishermen between Gold River and Tahsis. But of importance, the *Uchuck III* quite literally drops off sea kayakers.

By noon we're approaching the western shore of Nootka Sound. The captain yells down at us to bring our kayaks forward to a point beneath the booms. I slip into my fully loaded kayak, and the deckhands fit two slings forward and aft of my cockpit, the ship's winch engine revs, the booms creak, and I'm lifted above the leeward rail to the applause of my companions. With a smooth motion, the mate handling the winch swings me outboard—about twenty feet in the air—and gently lowers me into Nootka Sound.

I unfold the chart and lay it across the coaming. Ross Anderson comes alongside and holds a corner of the map into the wind. We orient the map and locate our position: we're in about 336 feet of water about 100 yards off Boston Point, a good four miles from the Pacific Ocean.

Though the water is reasonably flat, the afternoon winds are strong enough to force us to paddle close to the shore, traveling south into the sun. Ahead of us the hills that rim the sound begin to taper off, forming low-lying coastal plains that extend out of our sight as Point Estevan on the south and Bajo Point to the west. Together they form a broad bay that hourglasses in from the Pacific creating an entrance to Nootka Sound. We aim for the western side of this opening and the old summer Indian village known as Yuquot. Bligh Island, Cook Channel, Boston Point—our historical pulses quicken as we paddle the shore of Nootka Island. We're only a few miles from sharing a goal that began for both of us years ago.

My father was a sea captain; I was raised around ships, enamored with sea stories, voyagers, and passages to discovery. I've read every oceangoing book from Hollings Clancy Hollings's *Paddle to the Sea* to Joseph Conrad's *Typhoon*. I worked every ship I could, from longlining on halibut boats to reefing the topsails of the replica of Sir Francis Drake's *Golden Hinde*.

So too, Ross, throughout his life and career as a writer and reporter for *The Seattle Times*, has gathered multifarious bits of history, exploration, and discovery, culminating in his purchase of an original French "boot-leg" copy of Captain James Cook's *Chart of the Coast of America*. "I've always loved cartography, maps, and charts," he says. "I happened to come by one of Cook's original charts of the North Pacific from his exploration of 1779. The only place marked from San Francisco to Prince William Sound and Cook Inlet was Nootka Sound. For twenty to twenty-five years that was the only chart of the North Pacific, and Nootka became the

only port on the Northwest Coast, a port almost unknown 200 years later."

The latitude of Nootka Sound is 49° 35' 30". It is the latitude that Spanish explorer Juan José Perez Hernández would plot one August day in 1774, the latitude that would be the destination for Captain James Cook and his midshipmen George Vancouver and William Bligh. It is the latitude at which the European seafarers came in contact with the natives, ushering in the era of the sea otter trade.

Nootka Sound became what historians call the point of contact for the Northwest Coast. Over the next twenty-five years, more than 200 ships would drop anchor in what became known as Friendly Cove. Long before the Columbia River and Puget Sound were known, the Spanish, English, and Americans refitted ships here, grew gardens here, and vied for the sovereignty of this forested, deep-water wilderness.

Yuquot: the name is derived from *yukwitte*, to "blow with the wind." Prior to the arrival of the Europeans, it was the spring and summer residence of the Moachaht people—one of twenty interrelated tribes known as the Westcoast people, originally named Nootka by the European explorers, that live on the outer coast of Vancouver Island and Washington's Olympic Peninsula. At the point of contact, thirteen families from seven Tahsis Inlet winter villages summered here.

The first people of Nootka Sound lived a life that one could envy. The men set out for whales and fished for halibut, salmon, and cod. The women gathered berries, camas, and tiger lily bulbs, dried surf grass and sea grass into cakes for the winter, and collected the bountiful clams and mussels whose shells were tossed just outside.

Today Yuquot is overrun with brambles. From the crescent beach, paths break through the rampant vegetation and go up onto the old midden. The soil beneath is eighteen feet deep, composed of shells and fire ash, the detritus from at least 4,000 summers past.

The old village site is on a triangular spit that leaves

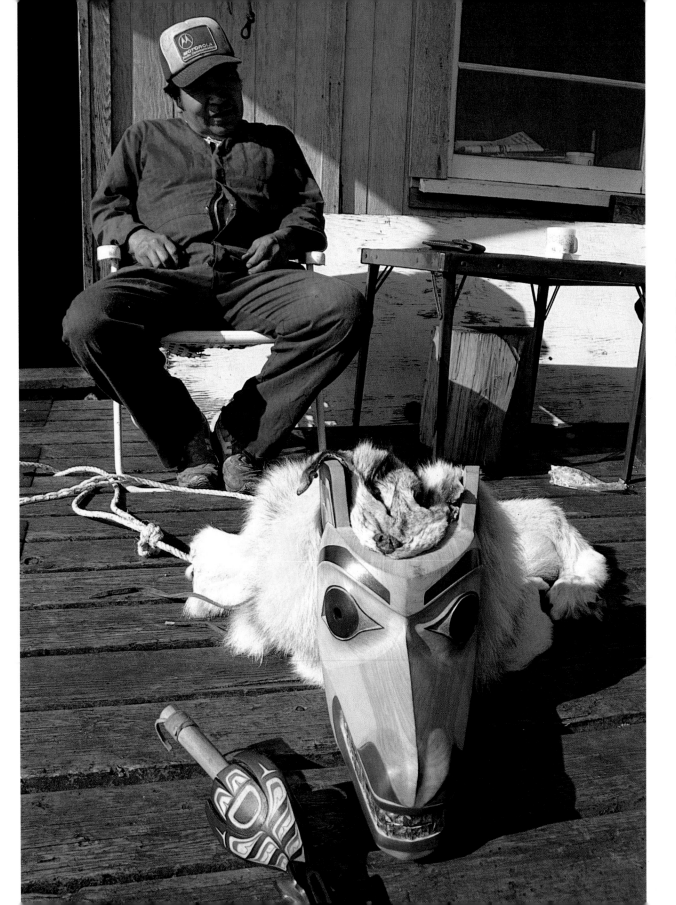

A father's pride in
the skill and
artistry of his son's
carvings shows in
the face of Ray
Williams. Yuquot,
Nootka Island.

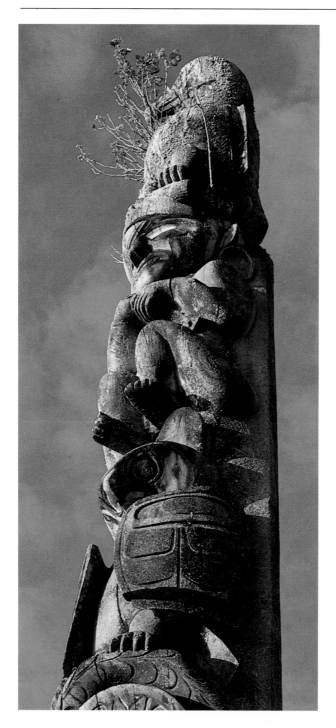

A contemporary (1927) totem, crowned with the returning forest, stands to the sunset at Yuquot.

Far right: A small tug, as if from a children's tale, tackles the log booms along the shore of Gold River.

the forest and runs flat and windswept to a series of rock outcrops and islets jutting out into the sea. On one side, a beach of small stones and scarred drift logs stretches westward for a mile against the force of the Pacific. On the other side lies the shelter of Friendly Cove. In the center is an old school yard with tumbledown goalposts, the school deserted and open to the weather. Across the grass, the substantial but empty church of Pope Pius V thrusts its spire toward the sun. Facing the cove, a north-south line of five small, boxy frame houses mimics the old plank house sites, their backs to the wind and sea. They too are abandoned, except for the new two-story, big-windowed home of Ray Williams and family.

Ray is the Westcoast people's caretaker of Yuquot. A big man with a broad, playful face, he looks strong and young though he is probably fifty. He fills the chair propped up against the front of the house, facing the sweep of the cove. As a young granddaughter's dark eyes peer out at me from the protection of the doorframe, Ray and I talk over a fee for our party to camp down the beach.

When Ray talks he uses short, slow, soft-toned sentences rich with the old language sounds: the *kw*, *tl*, and *sh*. We talk about the weather, the winters here, and we dicker on the price of our stay. I photograph his son's carved cedar masks and Ray himself. He tells me of the move by the government to make Yuquot and Friendly Cove a historical park commemorating the arrival of the Europeans. The Westcoast people weren't too enamored with the idea. "It wasn't a great day in our history," he says.

An outboard surges to life with a roar, and Ray's friends in from town run it briefly to make sure a repair will take. With the din, our conversation dies; Ray and his friends are going hunting. I've got dinner to cook. We settle on a nominal fee for our campsite and shake hands, as the engine starves and the sounds of the wind and the surf return.

The government did manage to place a rock cairn out on the last point with a plaque commemorating the

negotiations between Cook's onetime midshipman Captain George Vancouver and Spain's envoy Juan Francisco de la Bodega y Quadra. These negotiations became the Nootka Convention of 1792, a political sally toward the eventual British sovereignty of the region. The Westcoast people were never included in the resolutions. Fifty years after contact, the sea otter were hunted out and the ships departed, leaving European diseases, alcohol, firearms, laws, and religion to a bewildered and weakened Westcoast people. Their ancestral lands were taken, rights to freely fish their rivers removed, and Friendly Cove—too remote for Europeans—became uninhabitable to the Moachaht. All that remains today are the Ray Williams family and a plaque.

Dinner brings a discussion. We have three days to explore, but as a group we have different aims and abilities. We decide that Friendly Cove will be our base camp. From this location, we can slip outside for trips up and down the coast. And if the weather worsens we can paddle inside, exploring the islands of the sound.

In the morning, a north wind and clear sky draws three of us out, Tom Schwartz, Karl Weatherly, and me. Rounding the point and heading west along the beach, we paddle fast, enjoying the freedom of our boats that are now empty of camping gear.

The sport of sea kayaking has an exuberance that derives from an intermingling of the sea's natural energy, the paddlers' strength, and the fluid movement of our craft. Watching my friends meet the ocean, their kayaks bursting through the waves, I can see their exhilaration. Taking water over my own bow, my sunglasses speckled with salt spray, I turn my attention to the route ahead, enjoying our ability to explore outside the protection of the cove.

We paddle around the rocky point, and meet a cross sea of low swells, wind-driven chop, and waves rebounding from the rocks. The result is a confused pattern of

waves running in all directions. At times these errant energies meet and collide to form a momentary column of water known as a pinnacle wave. You don't really know you're on a pinnacle until you're suddenly rising up, higher than any wave yet encountered. While you're still rising, the waves just as suddenly continue on their respective courses, for the moment leaving you high and dry. I look over at Tom just as a pinnacle wave tosses him airborne, his paddle frozen in mid-stroke. He looks down where the wave had been, and his kayak returns, smacking the sea with a light-boat "thwomp."

A submerged rock surfaces ahead, and I brake with a quick paddle stroke, surprised that I hadn't seen the reef earlier. We circle the danger and slowly negotiate the rock garden off Maquinna Point. The wind is increasing and the sea is getting rough, so we turn back to a small cove where the mouth of a tidal stream leads inland to a saltwater lagoon. As we approach the outflow, we watch the surf breaking to our right along the beach to Yuquot. I'm not that accomplished at surfing in a kayak and still get butterflies on approaches like this. But the small headland on our left juts out enough to force the swell to refract around it and lose its punch.

One by one, we ride the dwindling surf into the cove. The forest of the headland blocks the wind and shades the stream. A sand beach borders the outflow, stretching toward Yuquot. Beyond lies a short, winding river. I pole my boat with my paddle through the shallows into deeper water, cedar water, water turned the color of tea by the oils of the wood. Overhanging firs are mirrored in the windless passage. Two mergansers, a green-headed drake and a reddish-brown hen, leave the upstream bank for the water, reluctant to fly. With each twist of the river the forest recedes, replaced by beds of salt grass. The channel broadens and turns into a shallow lake a third of a mile across. We paddle silently, a seemingly instinctive reaction to the sudden change from boisterous ocean to tranquil lake. In the morning this lagoon would host browsing deer, river otters, herons, and perhaps black bear. At midday it's quiet—just the mergansers shuffling along the reedy water's edge, getting some distance from these strangers.

The next day, we study the chart. The coast south of Yuquot looks even more formidable, westward facing and exposed to the full power of the prevailing swells. You can almost see the way the coast catches the wave action, the land pushed back, the weak strata eroded into small bays and even smaller coves. The stronger rocks remain as reefs and islets that act as a barrier, dissipating the sea's energy offshore. Between the reefs and the shoreline lies an avenue for safe kayaking and the potential for exploration on beaches seldom seen by contemporary man.

The crossing from Yuquot is two miles; the weather is calm and a mid-sky stratus sucks the color out of our surroundings. The sea surface looks oily and reflective, bulging with a long, lazy swell. I shoot a few frames of Tom and Karl, knowing the pictures may never be published; picture editors almost never choose a grey-day image. But grey weather is the other fifty percent of summer on the western coast of Vancouver Island, and we've learned to enjoy it.

Upon reaching Burdwood Point, we turn south and steer our kayaks into the backwaters of the reefs. One by one, we enter a maze of narrow passages alternately flooding with seawater and then ebbing to reveal a wainscoting of purple and orange sea stars. Squeezing our kayaks into little reef and rock enclosures, we find ourselves in a private aquarium carpeted with sea urchins and anemones and overlaid with bull kelp bulbs and fronds. Shoreward, the environment changes to little bays unaffected by the moderate swell. We ghost in, disturbing the kingfishers, noting potential campsites for another time.

Crossing back, the tide carries us through the entrance to Nootka Sound. The light on the point marks Friendly Cove and the promise of a campfire and friends. As so often happens in sea kayaking, I have no desire to head home. Looking back over my shoulder to the entrance, I wish that we were traveling for the

summer, running on the outside when weather permits, working our way along the coast from sound to sound, and taking shelter in places like Friendly Cove. For Nootka is but one of a series of sounds that penetrate Vancouver Island's exposed Pacific coast.

To the south lies Barkley Sound, a popular kayak destination. Part of Pacific Rim National Park, it is known for its Broken Islands, a pristine island group with a sliding scale of kayak experiences from quiet backwaters to the rough-and-ready front edge of the Pacific. North from Barkley, past the towns of Ucluelet and Tofino, lies Clayoquot Sound. Sea kayakers come here for the offshore islands of Blunden and Bartlett and the outside run to the fun of Hot Springs Cove. North of Nootka, connected by Tahsis Inlet, is Esperanza Inlet, the center of extensive logging activity. North again is Kyuquot, more wild than any of the sounds. This inlet leads outside to the Bunsby Islands, sea otters, and the "experts only" Brooks Peninsula.

Tomorrow we paddle to meet the *Uchuck III*. We will go back up Cook Channel to Gold River, and return to our own winter villages, to our own history. I grip my paddle and stroke to catch up with my friends. We skim the rocks at the entrance to Friendly Cove and paddle the last strokes toward a waiting fire.

◆

In the gold light of dawn, the Canadian flag flying her stern, the Uchuck III *departs Gold River and its paper mill that cloaks the head of Muchalat Inlet with twenty-four-hour smoke.*

SOUTH FORK

The Skagit River Estuary

OF WEBS AND CYCLES, zones and edges, methylotrophs and polychaete worms. From salmon fry to sticklebacks, bulrushes to willows. Harriers, hawks, and, in winter, eagles high in the cottonwoods. Beaver, deer, and coyote live here, and, if the freeway were not a barrier, black bear. These are ingredients of the Skagit River estuary—a salt marsh, a detrital soup, a rich stew of life rhythms percolating beyond the dairy farms and the distant hum of the human day-to-day.

The Skagit is a Washington river, born tumbling from the 8,000-foot glacial cirques of the North Cascade mountains, coursing down the steep, U-shaped valleys, flowing west. Growing with tributaries—the Cascade, Sauk, and Baker rivers—the combined flow swells to a volume greater than the Colorado before it leaves the foothills for its alluvial plain.

Unfettered by mountains, the Skagit curls and turns, meandering through 100,000 acres of rich farmland. The plain is famous for tulips, peas, and cauliflower. It is flat as a pancake except for a few

Left: The Skagit River estuary hazes with the first chill of autumn, and a kayaker welcomes the sun rising over the Cascade Mountains.

North Fork Skagit River

Skagit River

South Fork Skagit River

Skagit Bay

PUGET SOUND

—Freshwater Slough

Boom Slough

Deepwater
Slough

• Milltown

Steamboat
Slough

—Tom Moore Slough

Isohis Slough

· SOUTH FORK ·

THE SKAGIT RIVER ESTUARY

N

WASHINGTON

Dunlin rising, gathering, moving to feed with the ebb of the tide.

Overleaf: At the confluence of Steamboat and Boom sloughs, behind a line of alders and past a beaver lodge there is a backwater slough that hides ducklings and salmon fry.

isolated, curious hills, once islands, marooned by the 10,000-year continuous advance of the river's estuary.

Below the farm town of Mount Vernon, the Skagit divides into two channels—the North Fork, which transports its silt quickly west, intent on surrounding Ika and Goat islands, and the South Fork, the lesser flow,· which moves at a sleepier pace, branching into sloughs named Freshwater, Tom Moore, and Steamboat to build the estuary.

Milltown once was a small, bustling South Fork river stop in the logging and steamboat days of the late nineteenth century. Today it is just two houses, a population of four, numerous barn swallows, and, on the river side of the dike, a State Game Department boat launch.

The Skagit swirls and eddies into the launching area with the energy of spring. It is a good time to come, an early April afternoon. The alder and willow are blushing, taking on color, and the cottonwood buds perfume the slough with a honeylike fragrance. I roll my

sleeves above the elbows and shove my kayak, loaded for the weekend, into the current. While setting my spray skirt, I drift past a fleet of low, flat, plywood duck boats painted olive drab, stacked atop the floats below Ella's daffodil-lined river cabin.

"Did you see her hands!" old neighbor Tronsdal had said about Ella once, not unkindly. She does have big hands—hands that remain a symbol of the strength and size of this woman's life. Ella had toiled alongside her husband, shore logging (making up rafts of stray timber to sell) in the 1930s, and trolling for salmon—always connected to the water, the river. In her mid-eighties, shrunk by age and the world around her, she lives alone, alongside Tom Moore Slough, with her diminutive Chihuahua that wears a little knitted vest and shivers as a way of life.

A few duck boats are missing from the last float, evidence that Slicker and always Ziegler, who might love this place more than all of us combined, have gone

into their duck cabins for the weekend. I've suspected for years that these men could give a damn about ducks or duck season. I think they, like I, now come just to be out here.

Kayaking the Skagit, and estuaries in general, is unlike any other sea kayaking experience. I think of it as nature's nursery school for fledgling kayakers. Safe, shallow, and sandy-bottomed for the most part, the water is slow and manageable, except during the winter rains and spring runoff. Estuaries also offer lessons in discovery. The sloughs are narrow and interlacing, bending and turning, creating a sense of adventure and curiosity about where each passage goes. Above all, the estuary teaches the kayaker about a habitat of profound richness. Acre for acre, the estuary is the most productive of our environments, busy with the transit of marsh hawks, the darting of baby flounder, the shufflings of muskrats—activities that the inquisitive kayaker is privileged to observe.

Knowing the tidal rhythms allows the paddler to use the energy of the tide to advantage. The tide table for this day in the southern Puget Sound region looks like this:

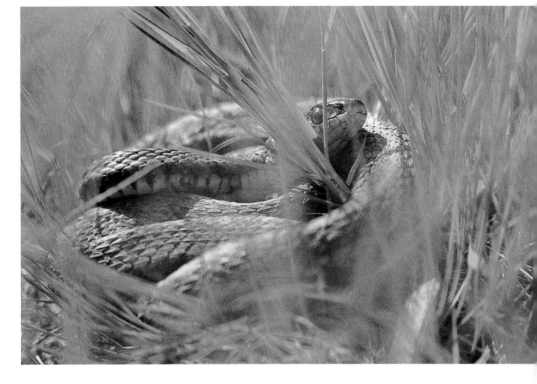

April 3 Tuesday Southern Puget Sound Tides	
HIGH Tides	LOW Tides
1:24AM 10.9ft **12:03PM 8.9ft**	6:57AM 7.3ft **6:39PM 0.4ft**

(For the Skagit estuary, which is north of this region, the correction is plus twenty-seven minutes for high tide and plus thirty-eight minutes for low.)

Ideally, if you put in at Milltown on a morning outgoing ebb tide, you have a free ride to the bay. Explore all day, and enjoy the two- to three-mile-per-hour returning flood to the landing. Today's tide is not a free ride but not so extreme as to leave me stranded. Over the years, I've experienced the many tidal variations, from thirteen-foot storm tides that inundate everything in the estuary, to minus-two-foot low tides that leave the tideflats bare for miles into Skagit Bay, prompting

the vivid term "sand prairies."

To learn the river, to know the pathways of the estuary—which passages cut through, which ones go dry at any given tide—you have to become a Skagit-scale Mark Twain. The topographic maps for the estuary lack the necessary detail, and local knowledge is too specific or too general. There's no way to learn this marsh other than putting in and letting the current take you down.

I paddle mid-channel of Tom Moore Slough, between banks lined with overhanging alder and groves of towering cottonwood. The river is cold and quiet, a moss-to-mud color, steadily flowing toward Skagit Bay and Puget Sound. My eyes scan the surface for snags, the banks for change, signs, or critters. A dusty Wonderbread wrapper hangs impaled on an alder branch about fifteen feet above the water, evidence of how high the winter floods crest.

After falling asleep in the summer sun, I awake with a companion—Thamnophis ordinoides—the Northwestern garter snake.

I am alone on the river. Aside from my duck cabin friends, about a mile down Tom Moore, these sloughs see only an occasional trolling fisherman, and duck season in the fall makes this place too dangerous for kayakers.

Water sounds. Something moves quickly; a river otter or muskrat, maybe a beaver, hides in the undercut bank. I slack my paddling and drift, folding my arms over my paddle shaft. On this early spring day, I can sense the marsh holding its breath as it gears up for a season of growth—the latent energy still in the ground, the sun, and the instinct of migrations.

About 300 yards below Milltown, on the right, a side slough cuts hard back and runs northwest. Newcomers wouldn't take this channel, especially with a tide as low as this afternoon's. But if you're a kayaker or canoeist, it's good to know it goes through from Tom Moore to Steamboat slough and the heart of the estuary.

I begin my turn early as the current sweeps me past; I paddle hard to swing around and up the stream. The waterway is shallow, at times forcing me to pole off the bottom and dodge sunken logs. For a third of a mile, I paddle and push my way against the current, my eyes level with the lip of the bank, layered mud, and exposed roots. The skunk cabbage is about a foot high but still just shoots, its leaves and flowers tucked and enfolded like sleeping bats. Winter grasses are faded blond, and last year's spirea, so fragrant, like pink lemonade in bloom, has dried to a dark rust.

This part of the estuary is known to biologists as the woody-stem zone of the salt marsh. It is the high ground, the least salty and more diverse in plant life. Its drainage sloughs are lined with a fine, deep, dark, bacterial mud packed with microscopic life. Its banks and bogs are habitat to bittern, coyote, and deer. Exiting this nameless connecting slough, shallow water gives way to the deeper channels of Steamboat, and I run with the river.

Camping in the Skagit estuary is illegal unless you have permission from land owners like Slicker or Ziegler. Even then there is little high ground to use. Years ago I began caretaking an old duck cabin on the west bank of Steamboat, where I hole up for the night. I check the chimney for bird nests and retire early for tomorrow's paddle.

April 4 Wednesday Southern Puget Sound Tides	
HIGH Tides	LOW Tides
2:24AM 11.1ft **12:53PM 8.5ft**	8:21AM 6.3ft **7:49PM 1.0ft**

Sea kayaking is a sport of many bags: a camera bag inside a rolltop dry bag, a big lens bag of the same type, a food bag, a clothes bag, a day bag, in addition to the rest of the gear—tripod, water bottle, and my Eternal Thermos—just to go picture-taking in a kayak at dawn. At six o'clock in the morning, I'm feeling particularly courageous. Everything froze last night; my kayak is candy-coated with ice. My gloves are poor excuses for pogies, and my past few breaths hang around me like tiny cumulus clouds. All bags packed, I slide the boat off the high bank and, balancing between kayak and shore, plop onto my cherished Thermarest cushion. Dragging my muddy boots in the current to wash them off, I slip them dripping into the kayak.

At forty minutes before sunrise, the surrounding estuary is a near-colorless tapestry of blue-blacks. Only an aura of lavender light over the Cascade peaks hints of dawn. Thrushes, wrens, and sparrows paint the darkness with their morning song, oblivious to my silent passage. I drift with the tide, keeping my body motionless while the outgoing current sucks me into Boom Slough. A riffle ahead marks the remains of an old steamboat, its keel and flat ribs coated with river silt. I drift safely by and into an open pondlike enclosure, listening to the birds, the drips and gurgles of the upland marsh, and the gnawing of the resident beavers.

I rudder toward the sounds, and in the half-light spot two mature beavers feeding along the slough edge. When they see me, they take to the water, their great tails slapping the surface in noisy defense. The

Overleaf: On a foggy morning, one greater yellowlegs among a pack of dunlin feeds between patches of last year's bullrushes.

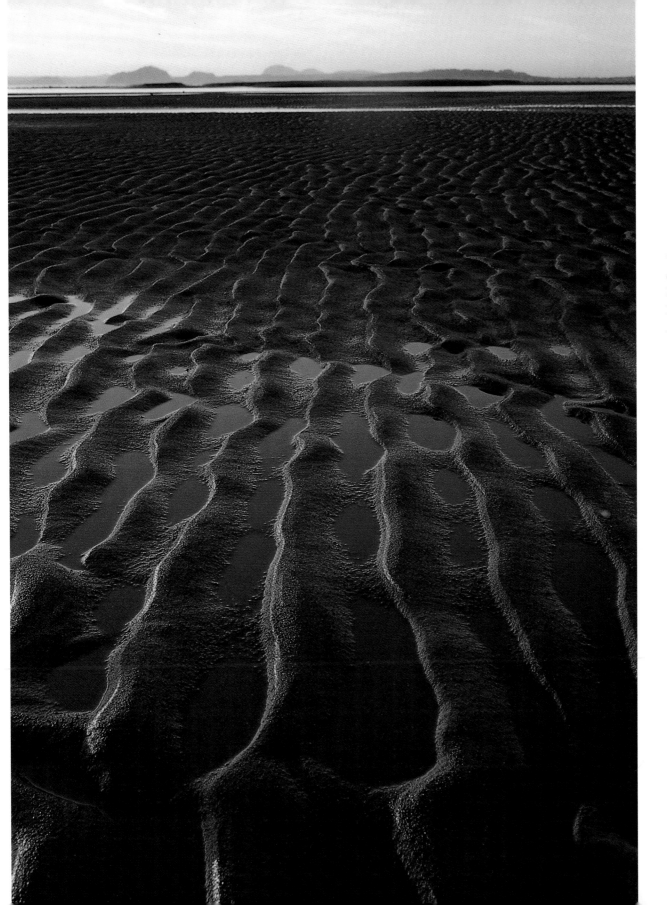

◆

*The sand prairies
of the Skagit flats
leading off to the
North Fork and the
La Conner hills.*

disturbance brings the eerie sound of approaching wing beats, as a great horned owl, white feathers against the dawn sky, flares above me and then arcs away in the heavy morning air.

In the west, the sun line descends, pink hues chasing the retreating night. I decide I'd better hurry if I want to reach the bay before sunup. Below the woody-stem zone, the forty-foot-wide slough is lined with winter-tattered cattail. About every sixty feet or so, a long-billed marsh wren in the early stages of nest-building stops to give warning at my passing. From the mouths of joining sloughs, pairs of mallards and mergansers explode into flight, and great blue herons en route to the bay silently veer around me and continue on to their choice fishing spots.

As the cattails and marsh wrens thin out, I paddle into a zone of braided channels and low sand banks peppered with tiny, yellow salt grass spikes. The change of scene from one of cattail corridors to sand prairies gives the sky a physical dominance. Overflights of snow geese and tight flocks of dunlin move above the margin of the bay.

The most visual and vocal of the Skagit's winter residents, the 10,000 pairs of "snows," as the snow geese are known, are one unusual, positive result of bad logging practices. Over the past 150 years, so much timber has been cut in the Skagit drainage that the resulting hillside erosion has dramatically increased the size of the estuary. The added sediment load created sand prairies and a perfect environment for salt grasses, primarily the three-square bulrush, a preferred food of the snow geese. With the growth of the three-square, around 1880, so the old farmers say, the first flock of approximately 200 snow geese wintered in the Skagit.

The snows are beautiful birds, about the size of the Canada goose but a golden white with black wingtips. They fly in Vs, heading inland to spend the day feeding in the farm fields and returning to the estuary at dusk for a night roost. In a week, this pattern will begin changing with the rapid growth of the salt grass. Then the snows will feed on the prairies—waddling lawnmowers snipping the fast-growing salt grass shoots, fattening up for the 2,000-mile May migration to Siberia, to nest and rear their goslings.

The sun is nearly cresting the mountains as I run out of estuary. Before me are Skagit Bay and Puget Sound swathed in a thin, low fog. Seemingly at the edge of the earth, I turn back and ground up on a salt grass bank. The tide is still on the ebb. I extricate my booted feet from the kayak and slowly roll to a standing posture. There is no cover out here: I stand in six inches of water that stretches away to infinity. Though I keep my movement to a minimum while I set up the tripod and mount the big 600-millimeter lens, the creatures around me are subtly distancing themselves from this vaguely hunter-like apparition. A harbor seal leaves first. A heron flies and lands out of gun range. The last small flock of geese honks away. But I know from experience one species will stay.

Dunlin are sandpiperlike shorebirds about the size of a fluffed-up robin on stilts. Like the snow geese, they are gregarious during migration and fly in large, dense flocks. Words can't begin to describe what goes on out here in the morning, at sunrise, when the dunlin take to the air. With synchronized flock movements, they take on the shape of a great, diaphanous amoeba undulating above the estuarine mud. At forty miles an hour, turning in unison, they reflect the first rays of sun.

Dunlin feed with the outgoing tide, skittering from one newly exposed mudbank to another, poking and probing their two-inch beaks into the mud for amphipods—the small crustaceans, 20,000 to a cubic yard, that thrive off the nutrients of the salt marsh.

A flock wings over to my lobe of earth and I begin to frame them, using the horizontal bands of last year's bulrush stalks for composition. As the fat dunlin hunt and peck, through my viewscreen they look like a musical score, a series of whole notes wandering purposely through a staff of bulrush set in the golden reflection of sunrise. Approaching to within twenty feet of me, the closest veer away, threatened, yet anxious to follow the receding tide and continue feeding. A sudden alarm-peep, and they're up and gathering more and more birds into a mass of feathers in flight across the surface of the bay.

My salt grass bank suddenly devoid of dunlin, I'm down to amphipods—not my preferred photographic subject. I pack my cameras, relieved by the respite from shooting into the dazzling sun. I've been out here for three hours and the ebb tide has long since stranded me. Not for the first time, I drag my kayak over the flats to the Boom Slough channel for the paddle back to Milltown and the hum of the human day-to-day.

◆

Left: Mount Baker dominates the Skagit estuary on a winter morning. The snow geese are up and hungry, moving back to sample the stubble of the farmlands.

SHI SHI

◆

The Olympic Peninsula Seashore

UNLIKE OREGON AND CALIFORNIA, Washington is not known for its dramatic shoreline. From the Columbia River north to the native fishing village of La Push, the coast is a 135-mile, more or less flat, wide beach, embayed at Gray's Harbor and Willapa, forested here and summer-homed there. But once past La Push, the topography begins to rise. Passing Cape Alava, the coast geology changes from recent Quaternary glacial and alluvial gravels, sands, and silts to the thirty-five-million-year-old marine sedimentary and volcanic layers. These strata, some soft, others hard, have been compressed, faulted, and inverted, and today, along the northwest edge of the Olympic Peninsula, the folded layers dip steeply northward to meet the force of the Pacific in an exposed cross section.

This northern corner of Washington's seacoast is made up of forty miles of storm-bound bays and high-cliffed headlands. Here there are scalloped, sandy beaches separated by sea stacks and arches so spectacular they are a surprise after the uniformity of points south, so intriguing they draw sea kayakers to dare the surf and storm in order to paddle through the rugged colonnades and camp on the deserted expanses.

In late July, the weather around Seattle had stayed

Left: *Surf kayakers ride the inner break—waves to eight feet—at La Push, Washington.*

87

Cape Flattery

Neah Bay

STRAIT OF JUAN DE FUCA

Makah Bay

PACIFIC OCEAN

Portage Head

Shi Shi Beach

POINT OF ARCHES

Olympic Peninsula

WASHINGTON

Cape Alava

Lake Ozette

· SHI SHI ·

THE OLYMPIC PENINSULA SEASHORE

N

hot long enough for Glen Sims and me to plan, pack, and drive to the coast. West of Port Angeles, we take State Highway 112 along the top of the Olympic Peninsula to Neah Bay and the ancestral lands of the Makah Indians, or "Outside Coast People." Following a dwindling set of dirt roads, we pull to a stop at Makah Bay near the mouth of the Sooes River. The surf is running from three to five feet. Once our kayaks are loaded, we time our paddle out so that we miss the larger waves and enter the Pacific.

Sims. Every time we paddle, at some point his melodious baritone booms across the water, like oil upon the seas of introspective thought, startling the scaups and in general lightening the mood of the moment. Glen Sims has a beautiful voice and is a strong kayaker; he still loyally paddles an old rootbeer-colored, scratched, and mended Mariner Escape. With Sims I can expect fast paddling, bizarre meals—the result of one-stop shopping along the road—and if the timing's right, an old ballad.

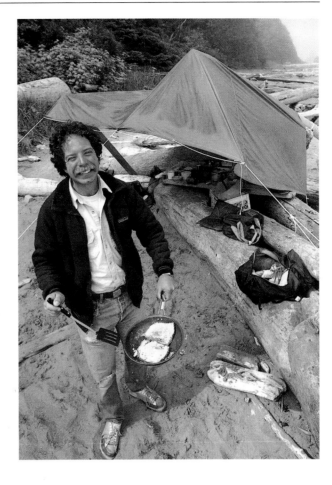

The inimitable Glen Sims prepares French toast at Shi Shi Beach.

> *When first I came to Liverpool*
> *   I went upon a spree.*
> *Me money, alas, I spent it fast,*
> *   got drunk as drunk could be.*
> *And when me money it was all gone,*
> *   it was then I wanted more.*
> *But a man must be blind to make up his mind*
> *   to go to sea once more.*

Our destination is the Point of Arches and Shi Shi Beach, once a Makah summer village site, now included in the primitive area of Olympic National Park. Shi Shi, pronounced Shī Shī, is a beach of mythic character, a northwest Shangri-La of golden sand framed by natural spires and majestic arches that act as collectors of the curious, seekers, and free spirits.

In the early 1970s, the consummate nonconformist Freedom and his wives, Sund the poet and Sybil the good witch, and others, packed in their wood-burning stoves and joss sticks over the old logging road to live on Shi Shi. They built whimsical driftwood cabins and lived freely in company with the negative ions. Today, they and their cabins have gone with the coming of time and the National Park Service, but Shi Shi remains the same—no road, no facilities. It is just as it was: mystical, beautiful, and wild.

I first visited Shi Shi in 1975, packing a full Kelty three miles over what is still, even in the driest August, the muddiest trail in the Northwest. I had checked and planned for low tides, and learned from a chance meeting with one of the Shi Shi people that I should leave the path early. In through the forest and down to a small bay, I then continued south from Portage Head alongside the crash of the Pacific. Teetering over the wave-cut benches, slogging through the soft sand edges of the beach, I sweated my way toward my first glimpse of Shi Shi.

If sweat is a main ingredient in the journey to all great places, I am glistening, living proof of Shi Shi's greatness. Fifteen years later, I vividly remember that first moment. I cleared my eyes, brushed back my wet hair, and saw a cavernous hole in the shaded wall of the headland. I walked into its cool darkness and entered a chamber created by the sea—a three-legged arch with Shi Shi beach framed in one passage, the Point of Arches visible through another. A wave surged into the grotto and I stepped back, waited, and then quick-stepped out into the sunlight.

Most every year since, I have made my way to Shi Shi, once on a lonely Christmas, another time in hot August when everyone on the beach went nude. Somehow, each visit is as fulfilling as the first, despite the collapse of the three-legged arch, the grandest entrance one could imagine to a Northwest wonderland.

Well he booked me on to a whaling ship,
  bound for the Arctic seas.
Where the ice and snow and the cold winds blow,
  Jamaica rum would freeze.
And the worst affair was I had no gear,
  I lost all me money on shore.
It's then that I wish that I was dead
  so I'd go to sea no more.

Our good weather has dissolved to a grey and threatening seascape off Makah Bay. Glen and I turn to each other with rueful expressions: we can always paddle back here if the beaches south prove too rough. But one hour later, it's back to blue skies and good moods, as we pass the old fallen arch and stand off the

north end of Shi Shi. Surf is hitting the beach hard, appearing to be six to eight feet high and breaking steeply—too much for us. We paddle south along the beach, looking for a calmer entry, watching the backs of the waves attacking the beach.

Closer to the Point of Arches, the east-southeast swell is blocked by the point's mass, rebounding through sea stacks. We ride into the beach on a perfect three-foot, slow-breaking surf. My favorite campsite is along the upper edge of the shore where the beach meets the coastal forest—it lies deserted. Glen and I carry the kayaks above the tideline and set our tent among the bleached drift logs.

The beauty of this campsite is its closeness to the point and its distance from the other campers. From our camp, Shi Shi stretches two miles north in an unbroken curve. With a sharp eye we can spot little clots of hikers arriving fresh from the trail, big with packs, larger than life in the shimmering midday heat. When they reach the beach they discover the backpacker's exquisite agony: sand. One by one, groups valiantly head our direction, only to fall short, lumbering into the driftlogs to find a site, set up a shade tarp, and massage their aching calves. Once they've set up camp, they continue toward us—barefoot, halter-topped, carrying cameras, holding hands—moving toward the point.

Come to the Point of Arches when the tide is low, when the sea stacks and islets are accessible. At low tide, the sand has filled in around the bases of the arches and stacks with a wave-ribbed floor, creating a sort of yellow brick road. There are arches to pass under, ramps to climb, and caves to amplify the sound of the surf. Rock corridors, their high walls hung with sagging starfish, lead off into tight passages. A turn one way may deadend at a dark, secret tidepool; another leads to a spray-struck Pacific vista. We watch the couples, the solitary strollers, one by one approach the edge of the stacks and disappear within until the evening tide flushes the explorers back up the beach to their camps.

Sometimes we're catching whales me boys,
   and sometimes catching none.
With a twenty-foot oar I'll stroke it around
   till two o'clock in the morn.
And when the evening shadow falls
   we'll rest our weary oars.
It's then that I wish that I was dead
   or safe with a girl on shore.

At 5:15 the next morning, our camp is enveloped in a light fog. Glen starts the stove and puts the coffee on to brew, while we carry our kayaks down toward the misty sea stacks. Within the hour, we paddle out day-tripping south to Cape Alava and the ancient Makah village of Ozette, long ago buried by a mud slide and today a valued archaeological site. By noon the day blossoms, making our return hot and windless—good picture weather. I shoot a great roll of the sea stacks, and I'm ecstatic as we return to camp.

About a half hour before sunset, we paddle into a small bay on the south side of the Point of Arches formed by flanking forest-topped sea stacks. Glen moves toward a "hole in the wall" arch piercing the base of one stack, to see if we can run it. We really like paddling through arches. Our pattern has been to sit off the arch, safely beyond the rocky shore, observing the wave patterns curl around the sea stacks and watching for sunken rocks to emerge as the bigger swells subside beneath the arch. If it's deep enough, calm enough, and clear on the other side, we run it. I drift toward shore, changing film, stopping once to paddle a few strokes away from the wavebreak, and drift again to secure my spray skirt. Then comes a shout.

I can't hear what Glen is saying; I just get a sense of the surprise and alarm in his voice. I look up from my camera and into the face of the largest wave I've seen all day. It is suddenly, instantly silent as the wave steepens, blocking the noise of the surf. The sun penetrates the wave, making it translucent. Glen, twenty feet out, is lucky enough to be pointing seaward, and with one swift

Left: Moments
before a rogue
wave hits, I take
a last photograph
while Glen scouts
the Point of Arches.

stroke he drops behind the advancing wave. I am not going to get off that easy: I'm pointing obliquely toward a rock-strewn bench, with no headway, a Nikon draped around my neck. I have time for one decision, two strokes, a desperate sweep, and I'm rising up on the wave's shoulder, my Polaris's bow batted back, broaching—parallel to the breaking wave. I lean into the foam, and catch a glimpse of my camera leaning with me. My paddle finds the back of the crest and anchors me. The soft chine of the kayak begins to slide along the front of the wave as I hang atop. I'm suddenly in control, rushing shoreward at fifteen miles an hour, buffeted in the welter of the wave.

I try to turn the boat, using the paddle to pull the bow back over the crest, but I can't. My head snaps back to where I'm going: rocks, a jumble of oddly uniform washer-dryer-sized rocks. But I'm rushing above them, maybe six feet above them, the foot of the wave filling in, flooding the reef just ahead. A rock larger than the rest breaks into my peripheral vision, and I visualize what my boat will do if I tag it. I involuntarily shut my eyes, and my kayak passes over.

The wave is five feet high now and slowing. I redouble my efforts to pull the kayak back over the crest. I think, "I'm going to make it." I lean way out and pull the blade toward me again without losing the fulcrum that has kept me atop the breaker. Before I can bump bottom, I gain the backside and sprint to deeper water. All I can do is laugh and shake. The wave that captured me may have been a rogue wave, a statistical probability stalking the world's oceans, according to marine weather expert K. E. Lilly, Jr.:

> *Waves on the ocean are made up of a large number of different waves having various heights, periods, and wave lengths. It is not surprising to find that waves occasionally reinforce each other, creating unusually high and steep waves compared to those prevailing around the area. In a storm-tossed sea, such waves will appear seemingly out of nowhere,*

roll ominously along for a few minutes, and then disappear.

Though I would be hard-pressed to call my sleeper wave a rogue, it very likely developed in the same way.

Waves are simple enough in definition. What intrigues me is their quality of surprise. Perhaps the essence of going to sea, whether aboard a 200,000-ton ship or a fifty-five-pound sea kayak, the mariner is at the mercy of the capricious power of the oceans.

To paddle the coast edge well, to extend one's paddling horizons to the world's oceans, the kayaker has to learn the sea as well as any mariner. This is the sustaining joy to sea kayaking—to really learn the ways of the ocean, to become capable of handling a variety of seas, winds, and anomalies like rogue waves.

I learned a good lesson. I had failed to pay attention to the outer swells, and I'd been too close to the shore break. But I had ridden that wave, and brought the boat and me back. Without looking, I know my camera is totaled. Purely as a formality, I place it beneath my spray skirt. Still I'm elated, soaring with the experience.

Glen and I come together, and he recounts that the last he saw of me my bow was high in the air. His memory of the shoreside rocks plunged him into the scenario, "How do I retrieve the body?" For a few moments our conversation dies.

We paddle out around the sea stack, the arch forgotten. As we approach camp, we check over our shoulders for the wave train and catch a little one into Shi Shi.

> *Come all you bold seafaring men,*
>   *come listen to my song.*
> *When you come in from those long, long trips,*
>   *I'd have you's not go wrong.*
> *Take my advice, don't drink strong drink*
>   *or go sleeping with no whore.*
> *Get married instead and spend all night in bed*
>   *and don't go to sea no more.*

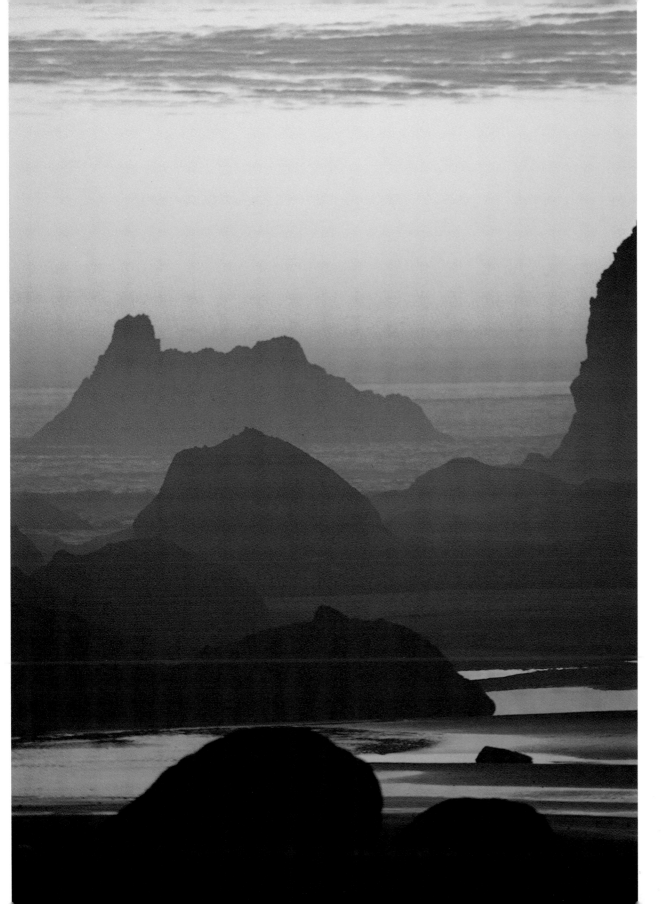

◆

Sunset, mist,
black rocks—
dinner goes
cold with the
fleeting moments
of a summer
evening sky.

EMBAYMENTS

◆

Willapa, Coos, and San Francisco Bays

THE PACIFIC COAST is indented with bays, and better for it. They provide shelter from the relentless wind and sea, and they lend a sense of permanence—though perhaps an illusion—to a land in rapid transition. Bays are odd in their attraction—passive certainly, so quiet they tend to be overlooked. While the headlands and capes have tourist overlooks and the great crash and bang of the surf, the bays usually have a heron or two in patient reflection and little towns backed up against the bordering hills. Willapa Bay in Washington and Coos Bay in Oregon are like that. San Francisco Bay was once that way, too. I've come to like these and other bays. They offer special kayak explorations into the backwaters of the land and sea.

Left: Willapa Bay on a late spring morning—a clear day for the oysters, marsh hawks, herons, and rushes.

WILLAPA BAY: Ordered Hosts

Virginia Graves looks mortified. Surrounded by the weathered artifacts of the Pacific County Museum, she protests my suggestion that I start my story with her casual reference to Willapa Bay's fifty square miles of mud. "I should never have told you that. Besides, we call them tideflats—fifty square miles of tideflats—you just can't call it mud." Virginia is a striking woman,

Left panel (Washington/Oregon coast):

PACIFIC OCEAN

North R.

Cedar R.

Willapa Bay

Willapa R.

101

South Bend

Raymond

Bone R.

Niawiakum R.

Palix R.

WILLAPA HILLS

Nemah

Nemah R.

Long Beach

Naselle R.

Naselle

Bear R.

WASHINGTON

Columbia River

OREGON

101

Center panel (Oregon coast):

PACIFIC OCEAN

101

OREGON DUNES NATIONAL RECREATION AREA

Coos Bay

North Bend

Coos Bay

Coos R.

Charleston

Sunset Bay

SOUTH SLOUGH NATIONAL ESTUARINE PRESERVE

101

OREGON

· EMBAYMENTS ·

WILLAPA, COOS, AND SAN FRANCISCO BAYS

Right panel (California / San Francisco Bay):

101

1

CALIFORNIA

MARIN HEADLANDS

Point Diablo

Lime Point

Alcatraz Island

GOLDEN GATE BRIDGE

AQUATIC PARK

THE PRESIDIO (army base)

THE BAY BRIDGE

San Francisco

San Francisco Bay

PACIFIC OCEAN

Oakla

1

N

tall and graceful, somewhere in her seventies. She came right out of her chair when I mentioned I was writing a book on sea kayaking. She and her husband, Biges Graves, built kayaks over twenty years ago to paddle Baja California—long before the roads made the access easy.

The museum's curator, Virginia walks me through South Bend's one-room storefront museum. Glass cases of arrowheads and old tools fill the room. On the wall, aged nameboards of lumber schooners hang alongside yellowed photographs of waterfront cedar mills streaking the sky with steam and smoke. The museum's displays tell of a pioneer struggle and a turn-of-the-century heyday when Willapa Bay and Pacific County were a bustling region. Salmon was in abundance, and millions of the bay's oysters were shipped to restaurants in San Francisco.

But it was timber that brought the boosters and entrepreneurs. Boomtowns rose as the timber was felled: South Bend, claimed by a 1904 Pacific County public relations advertisement to be the "Baltimore of the West," was a burgeoning town of 3,100 people—including five lawyers. Today, the town is the county seat and looks much the same as it did in the pictures, without the smoke and steam, and although the current number of lawyers stands at nine, the population is halved. The area is a backwater now, quiet and green. Fast-growing alders and the strength of the tide are subtly reclaiming the land once dominated by the lives of humans.

At South Bend, Coast Highway 101 meets Willapa Bay. The bay is large—122 square miles of tidal estuary, twenty-five miles long, six miles wide. At high tide it is a broad sweep of calm sea, but with the ebb the tidewater drains, leaving miles of rich, pungent mud.

My first encounter with the Willapa tideflats years ago was a tragedy narrowly averted. For some unremembered photographic reason, I walked out on a tideflat, making good progress until I stopped to frame my picture. Some twenty feet from shore, I became stuck.

Attempting to free one foot only caused the other to settle deeper. Sinking slowly above my boot tops, I first worried about my camera, then I began to wonder whether I was ever going to reach solid ground. Dignity was quickly giving way to self-preservation. I realized that the only way I was going to extricate myself, boots or no boots, would be to take the weight off my feet. I leaned forward to break the suction, canting my body farther and farther until I lay spread-eagled on the tideflat, my camera straight-armed out in front of me. I slithered to solid ground, coated from head to my still-booted toes with Willapa Bay mud.

What then is the attraction of kayaking Willapa Bay? Just south of town the highway crosses a series of rivers, one after another, three in less than three miles. Driving over the single-span bridges, you can catch brief, intriguing glimpses of what's upstream. This is the invitation to paddling Willapa Bay—not the open waters, but these winding streams where the tide pushes its way inland.

A legion of British gardeners could not have created a more ordered host of rivers—a total of nine empty into Willapa Bay. They are short as rivers go, some less than five miles long. Their names are a mix of native and pioneer: Palix, Naselle, Nemah, Niawiakum, North, Beaver, Cedar, Bear, and Bone. Flowing down from the Willapa Hills, their upland streams are typical Northwest sun-dappled creeks, cluttered with fallen timber from past clearcuts and enclosed by the canopy of the returning forests. But where their tributaries merge and the formed rivers meet the tide, the forest of uniform tree-farm second growth unable to tolerate the saltwater is set back from the rivers. Meadows of salt-tolerant grasses and sedges grow on the riverbanks, from a distance looking like well-kept lawns.

This river shall stay nameless—it is one of the nine, each similar, each different, each deserving a visit. This river, like most of its neighbors, is reached by a dirt road that cuts off from the highway and goes a short distance before it stops at a river landing. I arrive

too late at night to paddle, so finding a flat, dry spot, I set up my tent and turn in.

In time I adjust to the periodic sound of a passing car, its headlights flickering through the alder and young fir, its road noise penetrating a near perfect silence. A sound wakes me near dawn—someone or something is monkeying with my kayak on top of my car. I shine my flashlight and the beam strikes an owl, taking advantage of this high point to watch the clearing for prey. It moves like a man working a crick out of his neck, intensely focusing its wide-set eyes and jerking its head in sudden side-to-side movements. I watch until I am wide awake and ready to move. The owl flies as I leave the tent for the kayak.

The best possible launching spot is across roughly twenty feet of mud. But the ooze is firm enough to skate across and I push my kayak ahead of me. At the water's edge, I settle in and shove off the bank, quietly paddling upstream.

Away from the landing the banks grow steep, overhung with the rich growth of late summer grasses. My vision limited, I paddle to one side of the river to see across the flow and above the bank. At every bend there is a break in the vegetation where a smaller slough meets the river. As the bank folds back, I sight along the openings to the treeline, looking for the signs of pioneer homesteads. Before and during the boom years there were people here, living a river existence—working the oyster beds most likely—depending on the river for fish and the meadows for game. I spot a number of weathered posts, the remains of a dock, and go to investigate.

Getting out of a kayak on a muddy, high bank takes the thought and planning of an engineer. You must spread your weight, keep the boat balanced, and stay off steep banks so slick that a misstep means a sure dunking. I test the mud again and leverage up, one foot on semi-solid ground, the other on the centerline of my boat. Using my paddle for a crutch, I bring my weight on shore, mercifully keeping the water out of both boots.

The meadows are mostly grass and silverweed, a pretty, low-lying plant that is salt tolerant and distinctive for its leaf blades, fir-green above and silvery below. The presence of this plant is a sure sign of tidal inundation, no matter how nice a camping spot this field seems to be. I follow the rotted pier back through the grasses to the wall of the fir forest. Whatever was once here on the high ground inside the forest canopy—a home, a logging operation, a still— now is just mossed-over boards. Around and through the site, elk tracks by the hundreds flow along the protective edge of the trees following the course of the river. I follow their route over a treed spur and stop short of the tree margin to scan the next meadow.

There are two big-antlered bucks and a doe grazing not more than fifty feet away. I freeze and watch. Elk are big animals, with brown bodies and a gold rump patch, more solid and beefy than deer and far larger. One or the other watches across the river while the rest feed. It is unusual to see mature males in the open. They are a favorite of the local hunters, and hunting season is two weeks away. Suddenly I clap my hands, an almost involuntary reaction, and startle them back into the relative protection of the forest—to warn them about us. Feeling a little foolish, I watch them go. I scared them—a well-intentioned action of doubtful value to either of us. Sooner or later these bucks will fill a freezer and feed a family.

By the time I return to my kayak, the tide has reversed its course and I paddle toward the landing, watched no doubt by the puzzled eyes of the elk.

COOS BAY: Patchwork Quilt

The *Prince of Tokyo II* is a chip ship, a 38,000-ton, 667-foot-long cargo vessel designed and built for transporting shredded pulpwood to the paper mills of Japan. Negotiating the river bar entrance to Coos Bay, Oregon, she will spend four days loading her holds with 40,000 short tons of wood chips, the equivalent of 3,200 log truck loads, before returning to Japan.

◆

Left: The nine rivers of Willapa Bay wind to quiet ends among the boughs of cedar and the tracks of elk crossing muddy sloughs.

Once through the jetty, the ship negotiates the curves of the Coos River. She passes a number of active timber mills: Georgia Pacific, Oregon Chip, Roseburg Forest Products, and Weyerhaeuser—some manufacturing logs to lumber, most just exporting chips for paper production. Ghostly skeletons of deserted mills fill in the remaining shoreline, stilled by a century of fierce competition and the rapid depletion of Oregon's old-growth forests.

Beyond the piles of chips and rotting piers lie the old towns of Coos Bay and North Bend, their post-Victorian buildings showing decades of wear and hard times. The streets lie quiet. Vacant lots mark the remaining signatures of once proud structures. Second-hand stores are filled with books, tools, and old "cork" boots. And along Highway 101, the log trucks rumble toward the piers.

At the part of the river known as the North Bend upper range, the *Prince of Tokyo II* begins to turn with the assistance of tugs to make a port-side-to landing beside a mountain of wood chips. Stevedores take her lines, the hatch load points are matched with the great pierside conveyor belts, and the ship is ready to receive cargo.

Beyond the ship, into the haze of the river valley, lie hills covered with the raw earth of clearcuts and with random stands of second- and third-growth timber. A few remnant old-growth trees, known as relicts, punctuate the horizon. The scene is an old Northwest quilt, tired and still beautiful, a patchwork of history, industry, and played-out richness pieced together by the sloughs and tributaries of the Coos River.

The tidewater reaches over twenty-five miles up the Coos, past the confluence of the north fork—the Millicoma River—and the South Fork. Even into its headwaters, this is a working river: the hills are logged, the floodplain is fence-to-fence dairy farms. But the river is its own entity, patiently eroding here and building there. Its banks' vegetation of brambles, alder, and cottonwood overruns old landings that once docked

the paddlewheel steamboats.

Put-ins here are as scarce as environmentalists. But the South Fork has a public boat launch at about river mile twenty-two. I pull into the boat launch on an early July morning, to catch the fog lifting and the first glimpse of clean blue sky. It's mid-week and there's no one about. I shove off into a three-knot ebbtide mix of fresh river water and tide. The current carries me along, offering me an excuse to set my paddle down and trail my hands in the cool water. The low hum of a summer's day has not begun, and the sun has yet to crest the coast mountains to warm my back. The sweet, spiraling call of a Swainson's thrush awakens the riverbank, and a tractor starts up on a farm bordered by the age-old presence of great oaks.

My kayak drifts and turns at the gentle mercy of the flow of the Coos, my view panning with the swing of the bow. At times the river straightens, and my view expands downstream to take in barn roofs and fog settled in the ravines. With each turn of the river and swing of my boat, the light on the water changes, the advancing dawn adding color to its silver track.

An American flag droops on its pole over one farm between me and a recently logged hillside. This valley must have been logged about 100 years ago, for the loggers have returned in recent years to harvest the second growth. My upriver view is dominated by the cut-timber hills, and in time my thoughts are occupied by the controversy—the crisis of the last old-growth trees and the future livelihood of the local people. I am fixated on the term "renewable resources"; it bothers me.

In the Northwest, the logger has always been a romantic figure, a Paul Bunyan type who anchors much of the region's mystique and is the cultural basis of these forested coastal river valleys. But the romance is ending with the felling of the last tall trees—these 200- to 500-year-old giants are not renewable. In Coos County, an area of 1,692 square miles once covered with marketable forests, only an estimated 4,000 acres of

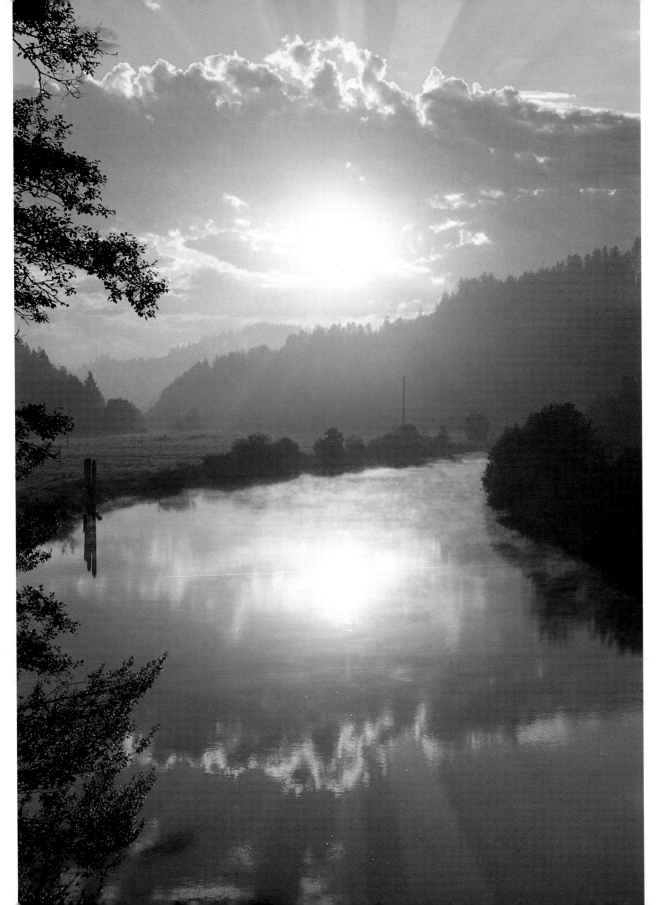

◆

Sunrise on the
Coos River.

old-growth timber remains.

It is unlikely that our children's children will ever see a tree farm of 200-year-old Douglas fir, because the dynamics of the multinational forest product conglomerates, so vulnerable to buyouts, foreign investment, and market uncertainty, indicate a return to "cut-and-run" logging of younger and younger trees. Now, as the third- and fourth-generation loggers of Coos County turn their anger on the environmentalists and nature itself, their local job base is shrinking with the size of the trees and they must sense that they too are not renewable resources. With the last of the forest giants goes Paul Bunyan, the romance, and the culture.

It is with some sadness and understanding that I paddle through the Coos River valley. I too used to be a logger—a choker and a timber cruiser. I can feel the dulling of the land's energy and the stubborn pride among its people. I grab my paddle to shake the train of thought. The sun now graces the river, as I approach the first of the towns and the river broadens into the bay. Mile thirteen reveals a ten-square-mile mudflat stretching off to my right, an estuary of channels to play in on a higher tide. I stay within the markers of Marshfield Channel for over a mile, paddling toward the waterfront of Coos Bay.

Five ships are in the harbor loading forest products. Among them is the *Prince of Tokyo II,* already deeper in the water, three days from sailing. Just beyond the Weyerhaeuser pier, I see three boys skipping rocks along the bay's edge. They are the only people I have seen who are not working on the river. Past North Bend, the current turns beneath the great 5,338-foot-long steel truss and concrete bridge that is the unofficial symbol of Coos Bay.

As I paddle out under the bridge, the sea begins to make its presence known. From the pilings of the ghost mills fleets of cormorants take wing, and a pelican lumbers by unperturbed by my passing. A northwest wind blows in from the ocean, slowing my progress. It is this wind that steals sand from the long beach that separates Coos Bay from the Pacific Ocean to create the Oregon Dunes, a forty-mile expanse of steep, blond, sand ridges and remnant forests ending at the northern shore of Coos Bay.

Two miles from the sea, the river makes a final bend past the fishing port of Charleston and the entrance to South Slough National Estuarine Preserve—the nation's first estuarine sanctuary. Two half-mile jetties—riprap arms of rock and rubble—are Coos Bay's last link with land. Still paddling the tail of the ebb, I pull on drawstrings, tighten Velcro, and check my spray skirt closure in anticipation of some standing waves. Arriving at the end of the north jetty, I can just hear the whistle of the sea buoy almost two miles out. It is then that I notice the fog, the first few low wisps swimming by, backlit by the golden afternoon sun. If I go any farther I may be swallowed up, isolated by fog. I turn with the roll of the swell back to Charleston, and the ten-dollar cab ride to my car.

SAN FRANCISCO: Kayaking to Baghdad

The closest I have ever come to having the wind rip a paddle out of my hands was underneath the north tower of the Golden Gate Bridge. It was my first time paddling San Francisco Bay, and like millions of seafarers before me, I wanted to experience the sensation of arriving beneath the Golden Gate. Fresh from the little cove in the lee of 500-foot-high Lime Point, I was solo, life-jacketed, and wide awake. I was making good speed, intending to paddle out against the tide beneath the span, then cross to mid-channel before turning to ride the current back into my favorite city.

But not more than 100 feet off the point, I got into trouble. The tide was swirling in from the Pacific, creating rips as it surged around the base of the bridge's north pylon. Whirlpools and eddylines ahead had captured all my attention, when a blast of wind descending from the Marin County hills struck me on my right side, caught my paddle blade, and blew me over.

My right hand lost its grip, the shaft pivoting

around, twisting my left hand to its full range as I struggled to stay upright. I knew enough to let the paddle go with the wind—just so long as my left hand stayed with it. Once the wind no longer had a surface to oppose, I returned to an upright if hunkered down position.

I had nearly capsized. It would have been sheer luck if I'd been able to execute a successful Eskimo roll—a technique of using body motion and a sweep of the paddle to turn right side up. But if I had failed, I would have had to exit the boat. Swimming in sixty-degree water and the turbulence of the tide, it would have been difficult to rig a self-rescue system before hypothermia began to take hold. This had been a close call. Between gusts, I got a full grip on the paddle and myself, and backed away from the eddyline to the protection of the point. Once my heartbeat had simmered down, I paddled forward to continue my journey.

Now I find myself, older and possibly wiser, once again paddling from the cove at Lime Point, bound for San Francisco and a breakfast caffé latté. Though the tide is flooding, the rips are fun, and the wind this time is only light air in the pre-dawn morning. It is October, a fresh autumn day in the making, but I am hoping for sunshine. With repeated glances past the San Francisco skyline, I will the clouds over Oakland to part in a picturesque sunrise. The weather gods give me just a piece of the sun, and it rises through a baywide layer of clouds. I photograph what I can, the city backlit in the morning haze that reflects on an undulating sea.

Joining the fishermen speeding out through the Gate, I move quickly, staying close to the Marin shore, taking advantage of back eddies and working the coves toward Point Diablo. An outbound tanker, the *Coast Range,* passes beneath the 225-foot-high span. I follow her progress as she returns to sea, the thumping vibration of her huge propeller resonant through the hull of my boat. Another ship is inbound on the south side of the main vessel traffic lane. The Coast Guard reports roughly 800 arrivals and departures of ships of over 20,000 tons through the Gate in any given

month—more than twenty-five ships like the *Coast Range* per day.

I literally look both ways before I begin to cross the channel. These ships cannot maneuver in the narrow, 4,228-foot-wide pass, and their speed is a distance-closing twenty- to twenty-five miles an hour. I turn and paddle toward mid-channel, soaring over the wake of the passing ships. As I near the bridge, the sound of a weekday rush hour is overshadowed by the neck-craning view of this remarkable symbol of San Francisco, its graceful orange cables strung from 740-foot-high twin towers. I notice a jogger, a tiny silhouette near mid-span, and surprisingly the person waves at me. I break into a grin and wave back.

San Francisco is a city everyone loves. Its nicknames

A mountain of wood chips dwarfs a "chip ship" at the Oregon port of North Bend.

bespeak a special fondness: poet George Sterling has called it "the cool grey city of love," Robert Louis Stevenson "the City of Gold," and William Saroyan "the wild-eyed, all-fired and hard-boiled, tenderhearted white-haired boy of the American family of cities." From the waterfront come "Frisco," "the Pearl of the Orient," "the Golden Gateway," and the "Queen City of the Pacific." President Calvin Coolidge called it the "Athens of the West," and for obvious if irreverent reasons, some call it "Shakey Town." But it is Herb Caen, the longtime columnist of the *San Francisco Chronicle*, who captures the elusive, quirky quality of this city: he calls it "Baghdad by the Bay."

No other American city strikes the newcomer with such promise or such heart. As I pass along the seawall below the Presidio—the old fort, once Spanish and now a U.S. military museum piece—the distant city skyline joins with the rooflines of Pacific Heights in an intricate and elegant jumble of architecture. The late-nineteenth-century and post-1906-earthquake Victorian houses are wall to pastel wall. They fill and lighten the hillsides, enticing would-be residents with their distinctive, colorful facades. Even the street names embellish the aura of the city: Java, Balboa, Cannery, Clipper, and Embarcadero.

Along the seawall, fishermen cast toward me. Behind them looms the great dome of the Palace of Fine Arts, the only remaining building of the Panama Pacific International Exposition of 1915. From my seagoing vantage point, I can imagine that era of simpler problems, tamer war engines, and far fewer people. I follow the waterfront of the city now given over to historic ships and marinas, and duck into Aquatic Park. I steer clear of goggled, capped swimmers lapping the expanse of the manmade boat basin and paddle for shore. Grounding on the sand, I make not a stir among the habitués of this waterfront park. Dragging my kayak higher, I cap it with the coaming cover, and sure of its safety I go in search of a latté, a croissant, and Herb Caen among the populace.

◆

Left: On my first paddle of San Francisco Bay, I head beneath the Golden Gate Bridge, into the wind and a near knockdown.

GUNKHOLING

The Oregon and California Coasts

GUNKHOLING is a recreational sailor's term for exploring a coastline. The word implies an unplanned itinerary and a surplus of time. It can aptly describe sea kayaking between Northern California and the mouth of the Columbia River. Kayaking on this coast is gunkholing by car along Highway 101, putting in where the shore gets interesting and the weather permits.

THE LOST COAST: Strong Breezes

"Dairy Queen, Buck."

"Buck" is Will Cooper's all-purpose nickname for any or all of us. The Dairy Queen is his link with the road-trip world. Slowed by the thirty-mile-an-hour speed limit of the gas and fast-food strip in Grants Pass, Oregon, our one-car, three-kayak caravan turns into the drive-in's parking lot. We step out into the ninety-five-degree heat of a southwestern Oregon August day.

Will orders a large "Oreo Blizzard"—a sort of solidified milkshake with crumbled Oreo cookies throughout. Cam Broze and I stand in the shade (we ordered the smaller version), failing in the heat to arrive at some disparaging remark on Will's penchant for this multi-calorie concoction. "I eat anything on

Left: Sun strikes the mouth of the Mattole River and sand blows against my legs. Even at dawn the wind sculpts the Lost Coast.

OREGON

PACIFIC OCEAN

Grants Pass

Crescent City

THE TREES OF MYSTERY

101

COAST RANGE

Arcata

Eureka

CALIFORNIA

Cape Mendocino

KING RANGE

Petrolia

Mattole R.

Punta Gorda

Eel River

Shelter Cove

1

101

Mendocino

PACIFIC OCEAN

Newport

HECETA HEAD—
DEVIL'S ELBOW STATE PARK—
THE SEA LION CAVES—

Florence

101

Coos Bay

OREGON

· GUNKHOLING ·

THE OREGON AND CALIFORNIA COASTS

WASHINGTO

Columbia River

Astoria

OREGON

PACIFIC OCEAN

Tillamook Bay

Garibaldi

Cape Meares—
THREE ARCH ROCKS

Oceanside

Netarts Bay

101

Newport

N

the road," Will had mentioned at our first Dairy Queen stop outside of Olympia, Washington—at ten in the morning. We old men in the shade nod knowingly to our younger friend with the body fat percentage on a par with dietary yogurt. His time for moderation in road-food dining will come soon enough. We check the kayak tie-downs on the Volvo, pile back in the car, and regain speed westbound on Oregon State Highway 199 through the first of the Coast Range redwood forests.

Cam, the co-designer of Mariner Kayaks with his brother Matt, and Will, a professional massage therapist, are serious sea kayakers who believe they will paddle all the coast that's worth paddling in their time. Today's twelve-hour, three-Dairy-Queen drive is a true test of such dedication. But our first destination is such a curiosity, the name alone is enough to get us past Grants Pass. We are going to paddle the Lost Coast, so named by the descendants of the sheep ranchers and timber men who 100 years ago effectively fought the encroachment of roads and people. The Lost Coast remains the last unpopulated, roadless wilderness coast of Northern California.

South of the Oregon-California border and west of the junction of Highways 1 and 101 lie over 400 square miles of little-known terrain with sixty miles of rugged seashore—a region of California that has remained rural to wild. Few have visited it; far fewer have ever paddled it.

As we wind out of the Coast Range at Crescent City and join Highway 101, it appears there's a good chance it will stay that way: fog blots our first view of the Pacific. The Lost Coast, like most west coast capes and headlands that breast the Pacific, is excessively rich in wind and weather. From the Columbia River south, the summer coast is swaddled in fog, the capes are windy—constantly windy—and it is decidedly cooler than Grants Pass. We travel south through Arcata and Eureka, subdued by the grey sky and the possibility that fog and wind will keep us on the beach tomorrow. We're 594 miles out of Seattle, some thirteen miles south of Eureka, when we leave 101 and cross the Eel River, which marks the boundary of the Lost Coast.

I had been here before—trying to paddle the Lost Coast last September and failing because of similar weather conditions. As we drive the remaining forty miles through the fog-shrouded ranchlands, I can smell the sweat of the tall meadow grasses blending with the salt of the sea. It is a California of yesteryear, dusty brown grasslands, rolling hills, evergreens in the draws, a few cattle, a long strip of deserted beach without a human trace. Climbing to one last summit, we drive the long, winding downgrade into the town of Petrolia.

Petrolia is not much more than a bend in the road—fifty people call it home. Its simple wood-frame houses, church, and school are sited on a bench beside the Mattole River in a beautiful yellow-green valley of meadows, glades, and forested hills. But this forgotten town has a ghost in the backyard: hinted by its name, Petrolia is the birthplace of the California oil industry. It was just two miles north of here that the first producing oil well in California was drilled and, in 1865, the first shipment of 100 goatskins of crude oil was packed out by mule train.

Mercifully, Petrolia was no Prudhoe Bay. There are no oil wells remaining, and there are no Dairy Queens. The only people drifting through are campers heading for the county beach five and a half miles west, which is our put-in for the Lost Coast.

We arrive in the dark. Our headlights reveal several tents rustling in the breeze. We stop short of miring the Volvo in sand, and settle for an exposed campsite.

Cam with characteristic understatement notes that it's a bit breezy. We climb through a barrier of driftlogs meant to keep motor vehicles from driving on the beach and follow the sound of the surf down to the hard sand. Though the surf is a slight two to four feet high, it is coming in on a steep beach and breaking suddenly right where a kayaker would enter the water. "Windy, too," says Will. Wind this late at night is not a good sign for tomorrow. We walk back and bivouac beside the car, as a chilly night settles over the mouth of the Mattole River.

I rise at dawn, cold and stiff, to see what the conditions are offshore. The wind is still blowing, ten knots or more, roughing up the surface of the sea, darkening the crests of the swells. The fog has moved away from the beach and lies a mile offshore, a 1,000-foot-high white wall highlighted with a touch of sunrise pink, stretching from Cape Mendocino to Punta Gorda. I stroll an immense sweep of grey-brown sand bermed with tufts of dune grass along its higher margin. This is the bay-mouth beach of the Mattole River, an environment pocked with the footprints of yesterday's wanderers.

By the time I turn and go with the wind it is whitecapping out past the break, and I realize the Lost Coast is going to stymie me again. Back at camp, after each of us has hiked out past the beach logs and pondered the wind, the fog bank, the surf, and the thirty miles of open coast to Shelter Cove, we decide not to go.

At 8:00 A.M. there are just too many cautions. We don't like the fog—we could paddle in it, but it's no fun paddling in a vacuum. The wind will probably increase throughout the day, building the wind waves and creating the potential for a difficult surf landing on an unscouted beach. And to make matters official, we have the warning from the *Coast Pilot*, the mariner's point-by-point, reef-by-shoal encyclopedia of current information on local weather, seas, unusual conditions, and navigation for all U.S. coastal waters. For the Pacific Coast, its terse prose describes Punta Gorda, on our intended route, two miles south:

A high, bold, rounding cape 11 miles south of Cape Mendocino, the seaward face rising to about 900 feet (Punta Gorda) is bare of trees, except in the gulches. The grey rectangular structure of an abandoned lighthouse, 25 feet high, is south of the point. For over 1.5 miles north and 2.0 miles south

of the point, the beach is bordered by numerous rocks and shoals extending in some cases 0.6 mile offshore.

The wind, sea, and currents off Punta Gorda are probably as strong as off any given point on the coast; frequent and strong tide rips have been noted. Many times when the weather at Shelter Cove is clear and calm and the sea smooth, both the wind and the sea will pick up as Punta Gorda is approached, until just north of this point where strong breezes to moderate gales will be experienced. At other times clear weather south of this point will lead to fog north, or vice versa.

"Or vice versa." Silently eating our granola, we are wondering if we should attempt to do it, but the boats stay lashed to the Volvo. To salvage something from our decision and see what we can of the coast, Cam mentions being curious about the Punta Gorda lighthouse, abandoned back in 1951, and we decide to hike to it. The downwind leg is through low dunes and past fenced Mattole Indian archaeological digs. At times we walk the beach, dodging the swash of the waves, watching the reefs and the sea beyond. At one point there is a perfect bay formed by the low reefs that is not apparent on the topographic maps. It would allow a safe, even dry, landing. Cam comments that at a higher tide and with a heavier sea, the waves would sweep right into this bay. Nonetheless I keep watching the possible route around the point, aching at the proper but frustrating decision not to paddle. And still the wind increases.

When we reach Punta Gorda, we decide to climb up over the grassy ridge. We spook cattle out of the sheltered gulches and watch the chilly return of the fog. Before we can walk the remaining half-mile to the squat little lighthouse, the wind begins tearing the tops off the breaking waves.

Back at our car, we follow Highway 101 north into Oregon, out of the wind, gunkholing up the highway of kitsch.

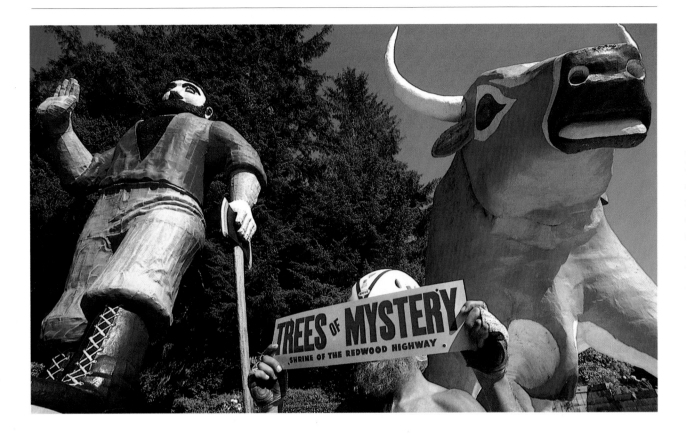

Paul Bunyan,
Babe the Blue Ox,
and Michael
the shy cyclist
contribute to
the kitsch of
Highway 101.
Trees of Mystery,
California.

HECETA HEAD: Roadside Attraction

Highway 101, the "Redwood Highway," is the home of burlwood tables, myrtlewood bowls, and redwood trees, the Trees of Mystery, Trees of Confusion, and the Tour-Thru-Tree, the world's tallest totem pole, the world's shortest river, Twenty Miracle Miles of craft shops, Tillamook Cheese, and the Sea Lion Caves. The Sea Lion Caves, a tourist site featuring a 1,500-foot-long sea cave filled with honking, barking sea lions, are just north of Florence, Oregon. This one attraction must consume one-third of the state's pulp tree production just to maintain the prolific bumper sticker marketing. We have seen the bumper ads our entire trip, but now in the afternoon of our third day, 171 miles into Oregon, they are coming thick and fast.

Highway 101 has left the dunes above Coos Bay, rising with the basalt cliffs that form Heceta Head. As 101 narrows, hugging the cliff, cars and campers brush by one another, everyone straining to get a new perspective on the ocean breaking below. It is here, just beyond Sea Lion Caves, that the most famous Kodak picture point of the Oregon coast commands people to careen their cars into the turnouts. The photographer of each family becomes quite serious and stands into the wind, aiming his or her camera toward Heceta Head, its lighthouse commanding a craggy promontory, the surf exploding beneath it. We are no different. The view is timeless and evocative. As we continue along the precipice, signs for Devil's Elbow State Park begin to slip by. At the entrance to the park, we drive down to

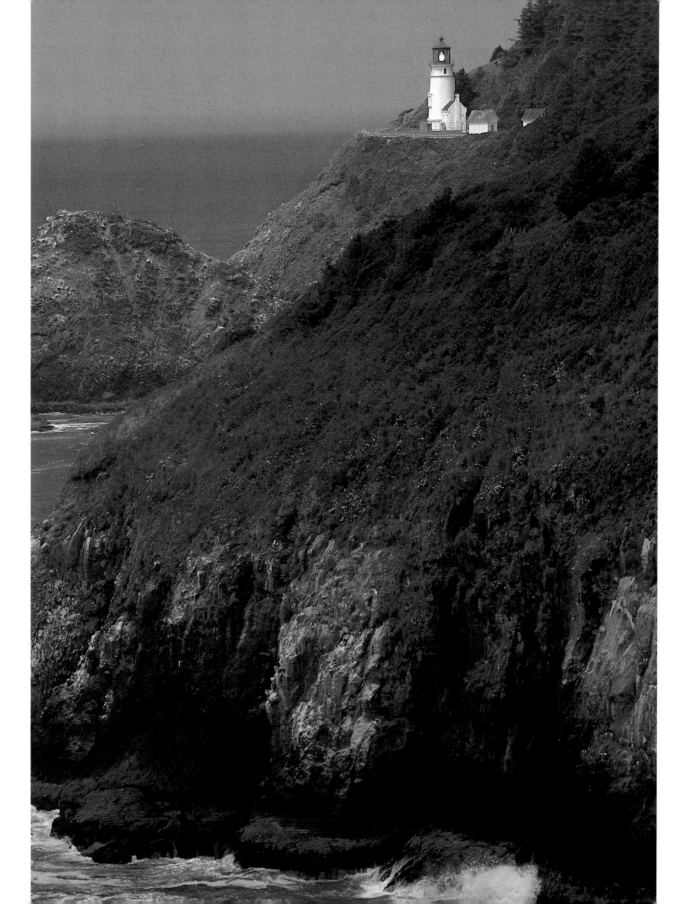

Heceta Head light, the most photographed of the six lighthouses on the Oregon coast.

a cove, some polite surf, and one of the best paddles on the Oregon coast.

There is something so satisfying about dragging your kayak across the sand to the water's edge, putting on your spray skirt and life jacket, and paddling away from the last dry margins of shore. Each and every time I get into a kayak and quickly travel out to where, as a child, I never expected to be, I feel a personal excitement that strengthens my strokes and drives my kayak through the swells.

One by one we negotiate the surf, which is not more than three feet high in this protected bay. Will takes a couple of waves over the bow that drench him. Cam and I miss the breakers by weaving through a hole in the surf line caused by the uneven ocean bottom. If you want to get away from a beach dry, as many of us do, there are ways. If you read a beach, watch the break, find its weakness, sense the rhythm of the wave sets—you just might do it. At Devil's Elbow, as the swell comes ashore it "feels" the bottom, and its friction slows and steepens the waves until they break.

Cam and I head for a deeper area of the cove. Here the approaching waves continue on without breaking for an extra fifteen or twenty yards, while the same waves on either side rush in over shallower water, break, and slow. We scoot through the resulting gap and paddle quickly to beat the next wave, dry as a bone. A sputtering Will is out beyond the shore break, and we wait while he repairs the damage. I scan a hazy sky and an almost windless sea. What a difference a new day, a few hundred miles, and a less exposed cape make.

We can run north or south. Either direction is not a long paddle—about a mile and a half. But the headland, this gigantic set of rock buttresses splaying into the sea, riddled with caves and arches, lures us to explore. Without much further conversation, we decide to head north through a small arch that opens to a cave in one direction and a safe exit in the other. The Heceta Head lighthouse flashes 205 feet above us, a million-candle-power beam visible for twenty miles.

One by one we negotiate a narrow pass, a channel of confused sea, first Cam, then Will, then I. We try to establish whether there is a reef below us by paddling in place, watching a big set of waves move through, and scrutinizing the passing crests for anything solid visible in the trough. We play follow-the-leader through the rock gardens for the next hour. When we reach the end of the headland, we turn and retrace our path, running the gauntlets and arches until we stand off Sea Lion Caves. We look up at the tourists a good 300 feet above us staring down.

The cave is amazing: it is actually a huge tunnel with a cavernous, chambered opening to the south and a smaller portal through the headland to the north. A prodigious number of Steller's sea lions have taken shelter here for thousands of years. We can't go in the cave—it's the sea lions' domain. We also keep well back from the outer rock ledges, so we do not spook the animals. Approaching the end of the cliffs, we turn in unison, paddling together in continued good weather. For a moment I wonder what's happening at Punta Gorda, but that is for another time, another attempt.

"Dairy Queen, Buck!"

CAPE MEARES: Three Arch Rocks

Why is it that the average Oregon coast restaurant seems to be intent on thickening its clam chowder to the consistency of bread dough? Each year I travel the highways, the chowder gets a little thicker: crackers are superfluous, steak knives an eventual necessity. Poor Will. Poor me. I also subscribe to Will's precept of eating anything I want to on the road: chicken-fried steaks, caramel milk shakes, Denver omelets. Will is incorrigible—he orders onion rings so deep-fat-fried you can hardly find the onion. The Oreo Blizzard is a veritable health food by comparison.

After traveling north to Cape Meares, covering much of the 374-mile length of Oregon's part of Highway 101, we stop at the town of Garibaldi and pull up at a seafood restaurant. During our meal, Will and I discuss the relative merits of a chain or franchise restaurant versus the mom-and-pop drive-in. It's tough these days to find anything along the road worth eating. There seem to be numerous trends, none of them good, to my mind. The most obvious is that the McDonalds and Dairy Queens are forcing the small-town mom-and-pop drive-ins out of business. As they struggle, the small diners have cut corners to the extent that you can hardly trust the egg on your plate. Along 101, there is a steady disappearance of real food: you're offered nondairy creamers, fake butter, and imitation sour cream—a true sacrilege. Ice cream is made from a mix, hamburgers are laced with vegetable filler, and everything is either salted or sugared into inedibility.

My clam chowder stares back without a response. Will is having french fries and gravy. We are losing daylight and have yet to find a campsite. After we beg a Xerox copy of the local chart from the Coast Guard, we pilot the Volvo out to Cape Meares. In the dark and the fog, we camp beside a back road. The following morning, we drive to our put-in on the southern side of the cape at the beach town of Oceanside.

Cape Meares is flanked on either side by saltwater lagoons; the larger to the north is called Tillamook Bay, the smaller is Netarts Bay. Cape Meares would do Ireland's coast proud. Vertical cliffs to 640 feet isolate a series of bays and caves for two miles. And off the cliffs, a half-mile out to sea, Three Arch Rocks promises new paddling adventures.

Our put-in is a small cove on the southern, protected (in summer) side of a large point. As at Heceta Head, the waves are three feet, and we ride out on what must be a riptide channel to the Arches. There we encounter some of the most monumental deepwater architecture we've seen.

What strikes you about Three Arch Rocks is that they have their own kind of symmetry. The first passage is 100 feet long and forty feet high, the second 100 feet high and forty feet long. The third arch is so like a major freeway tunnel you'd swear it had been

Right: *Each arch is a different experience, depending on the tide height, sea swell, and hidden reefs. Will Cooper negotiates a small free-standing arch with a tricky set of entry reefs on the north side of Cape Meares.*

engineered: 300 feet long, sixty feet wide, forty feet high, and straight as an arrow. In all three, there are no visible reefs, no jutting buttresses or side caverns, just hundreds of whitewashed perches for birds: pigeon guillemots, a charcoal-colored seabird with white wing bars and flashy red feet; common murres, the species that was the most impacted by the *Exxon Valdez* spill; and, though not in the caves but nesting nearby and fishing just off my bow, the tufted puffin, the rare little racer of the seas, always seen with several little fish sandwiched in its beak.

Paddling around these islets, it is obvious that every nook, ledge, lee, and even the wind-exposed northern sides of these rocks are life-giving sanctuaries. Gulls predominate, and pelicans also gather here. Cormorants line the crowns of the rocks closer to the water, and sea lions by the hundreds bark in casual alarm.

As long as I do not approach too close and cause a sea-lion-pup-flattening stampede, I can edge into their presence, usually drawing forth a few younger males to sniff me out. If you are downwind from their perch, the animals will try to get downwind of you, making long drawn-out snorts. About ten youngsters, long necks craning, come out of the water to their shoulders, bunching behind me and vying for the spot that gives the strongest whiff of my scent. They bark in what must be a pungent chorus of sea lion tunes but cause no alarm. I allow the drift of the current to pull me away from their rocks.

I race to catch up with Will and Cam as they approach the main part of the headland. From cove to cove, we check for reefs and then paddle in. As the waves steepen and roll beneath us, each swell sends a breeze past us seaward, reminding me of the wild ride off Shi Shi Beach. I wonder if my alertness to danger has improved since that episode. But there will be no rogue waves today, just perfect arches and an occasional puffin flying by like a giant bee. Cam is anxious to try some surfing back at the Oceanside beach, so we turn for the surfing and inevitable dunking and home.

◆

Left: Steller's sea lions and suburbia meet along the Oregon coast, at Three Arch Rocks, Oceanside, Oregon.

ANACAPA CROSSING

◆

The Santa Barbara Channel Islands

THE HOUSES EDGING the Santa Barbara Channel are going for nothing less than a million up. At Oxnard, a breakwater has been added and a dense canalside development fills the harbor. Just past the suburbanized Coast Guard station lies a small public beach, unadorned except for a line of cormorants atop the breakwater, wings hung out to dry.

I pull my car to a stop and become a player entering the rhythm of the Southern California dawn: trim runners in neon lycra jog by wired to their Walkmans, gardeners' pickups pass en route to their first appointments, clean, waxed, and unhurried. The waterway is already active with pleasure craft skipping out on another fine, sunny Friday—everyone here expects good weather as if it is a right. The Southern California mystique pervades even this last remaining strip of undeveloped shore.

Not knowing whether I'm an anachronism or the wave of the California boating future, I heft my kayak to join the group bound for Anacapa Island. Between

Left: Sea kayakers make an easy passage beneath the broad volcanic arch of Anacapa, edged with preaning pelicans and weary cormorants on the protected south side.

CALIFORNIA

Santa Barbara

●Ventura

●Oxnard

●
Gina (offshore oil rig)

Santa Barbara Channel

San Miguel Island

Santa Cruz Island

Anacapa Island

Santa Rosa Island

PACIFIC OCEAN

Santa Barbara Island

· ANACAPA CROSSING ·

THE SANTA BARBARA CHANNEL ISLANDS

N

San Nicolas Island

trips from the car to the beach, I meet the other paddlers; we exchange names and size each other up. We are five men and one woman, ranging in ages from twenty-eight to fifty-four. Richard and Mark are engineers, Peter sells for a multinational printing firm. Our guides are Joanne Turner and Doug Schwartz, owners of Southwinds Sports Resource. Both appear to be at ease with the group, the weather, and the crossing.

Doug calls us together and outlines the three-day trip: our destination is Anacapa, one of the smallest of the eight Channel Islands and one of four islands that comprise the Channel Islands National Park. The name of the island is derived from the native Chumash word *eneeapah*, meaning deception. Anacapa is just that—it is one of nature's stage props. Just over three miles long, the island looks large on the ocean horizon, its highest hill nearly a thousand feet. But in reality, Anacapa is three joined islets and averages only a third of a mile in width. Trending west, it is dwarfed by nearby Santa Cruz Island with ninety-six square miles, Santa Rosa Island with eighty-four square miles, and fourteen-square-mile San Miguel Island. Together, the four form the northern chain of islands that enclose Santa Barbara Channel.

Today we will paddle the thirteen miles across the channel to camp on Anacapa, and the following day we will circumpaddle the island. On Sunday, weather permitting, we'll paddle back. Steady winds rising in the afternoon, ship traffic, possible fog, and lots of exercise are in store for us. Joanne goes over the safety factors: we learn a basic set of hand signals, and we are cautioned to stay together and wear our life jackets at all times on the water.

As I listen to Joanne and Doug, I like the way these two have put the trip together—it will be safe, because of their local knowledge, judgment, and skill and the fact that they require all of us to have ocean and surf experience, and simple, with each of us being responsible for his own food and kit. Then Joanne and Doug, unlike most outfitters, actually will have time to share

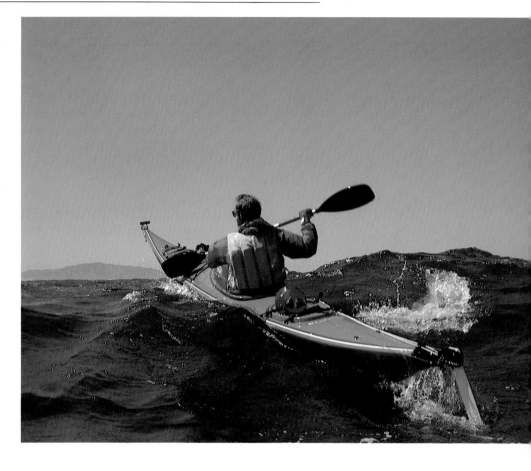

the relaxing aspects of the trip. We finish loading, don life jackets, and shove off.

This is to be a long crossing: Doug anticipates about three hours of open ocean paddling. This morning, it's sun at our backs, light winds on our right cheek, and a four-foot westerly swell. Free of the traffic at the jetty entrance, I paddle with the pleasant satisfaction of once again being on the sea. My shadow runs ahead of me across a deeply blue approaching wave, as my Polaris settles into the trough with little fuss. The sea surface is busy but there's no spray, and my apprehension about the big crossing, bad weather, and new people drops away with every stroke.

The Santa Barbara Channel at mid-afternoon: Richard Cheek paddles toward the elusive shore of Anacapa Island.

Joanne lets out a sharp "whoop" for attention, then points at a big smudge on the horizon known as "Gina," Unocal's offshore oil rig, four miles out to sea. In line with distant and not yet visible Anacapa, Gina is our fixed navigational aid for the next hour, our compass heading that in time tells us we are drifting south. Doug calls a course change, pointing us in a more northerly direction, and then settles back to talk to me, paddle-to-paddle, about the risks of kayaking to the Channel Islands.

"The wind averages seventeen to twenty-one knots in the spring—that's force five on the Beaufort scale, twenty-four hours a day," Doug says. "Wind waves can reach eight feet out here easily, on any afternoon. By summer, it tapers to the yearly average of eleven to sixteen knots, and September is a calm force three at seven to ten knots. That is precisely what we've got this morning. But the real fear on this crossing is not the wind but the fog. All through the summer, fog can blanket this channel and we won't go. We'll sit on the beach until it lifts."

I wonder, "Why not use a compass?" And Doug answers my unasked question: "It's the ships that stop you. Over thirty big ships pass between Anacapa and Oxnard daily—container ships, tankers, and aircraft carriers—all moving at twenty to thirty knots. In the fog they are deadly. You can't hear one of those container ships on a collision course—they are absolutely silent."

And so are we. Two hours out, midway, we stop to let a bulk carrier sailing under a Greek flag pass at 300 yards. There is no indication that the men on the bridge have seen us, as the ship rumbles by.

Morning turns to afternoon, and we are bow on to Anacapa. Cliffs ring the island. There are no beaches or safe harbors to speak of. Our eastern islet destination is meadowed, golden in the September sun. A lighthouse flashes on the closest promontory, and we paddle toward this vision.

The wind, slowly rising since mid-channel, has reached a steady fifteen to twenty knots. A strong set of sea waves with breaking crests moves in from the west,

and we begin turning to meet the big ones. I check my paddling partners—everyone still has a smile. Richard gets slapped with a breaker and howls, as the seawater find its way beneath his spray skirt.

The lighthouse seems to be getting no closer. At first I think it's just the game of distance versus the desire to get there, but not more than two miles off Anacapa we discover we are virtually standing still. Joanne steams up, her bow clearing the crests to mid-coaming. She gives a yelp for attention and signals a turn to the west—into the wind and a current we had suspected since passing Gina but whose strength we'd had no idea of until now. At rest, we are being carried by the current past the southeast end of Anacapa at a good three knots. We paddle a hard hour toward the island in a ferry glide, using the wind to sail us like a close-hauled sailboat, until the rough sea and the bite of the current lessen in the shadow of Anacapa's cliffs.

We gather in a small, rounded bay, not more than 100 feet in diameter and rimmed on three sides by 150-foot-high cliffs. Our harbor is scant protection, the sea waves scudding by no more than three boat lengths away. We congratulate ourselves on our long, but exhilarating paddle; our muscles ring with their sudden stillness.

Landing at Anacapa is the next hurdle. There is no beach, no rocky reef—just walls of ancient lava rising to the sunlight. Doug and Richard have landed at a pier cemented to the west side of the rock and have grabbed a ladder and hauled themselves up to the deck. They throw down carabiners and rope rigged together as a rudimentary pulley system. Joanne hooks on my boat's bow and stern, and on a rising wave I grab the ladder and climb up, my boat hoisted up behind me.

The national park ranger descends the steep staircase to give us our orientation. He warns us about smoking, seeming surprised and pleased that no one does, and tells us about the island. Anacapa is the most visited of the four islands that make up Channel Islands National Park—one of the least visited parks in the nation. Since the days of the Spanish, man has looked to the Channel Islands for opportunity. The sea otters that once inhabited the area in abundance were hunted to extinction. The ironwood forests that filled the island's draws were cut. Goats were introduced, as well as sheep, cattle, horses, pigs, rabbits, and other environmental loose cannons. With most endemic species munched to oblivion, the denuded islands supported a few ranches and sheltered occasional hermits. They even acted as convenient targets for the military.

In 1938, the preciousness of these last wilderness islands, so close to but so distant from the burgeoning California culture, was recognized. Anacapa and the tiny, mile-square Santa Barbara of the southern Channel Islands were first designated a national monument. And in 1980, they became a national park, adding Santa Rosa and San Miguel islands.

We thank the ranger for the information. One senses he and his family will not make a career out of lonely Anacapa, as the sound of his footfalls up the stairs is lost in the vigor of the wind.

The only campsites allowed on Anacapa are a third of a mile into the wind. To carry our gear up the 144 steps to the tablelike meadow, Joanne suggests we balance our drybags on our paddle shafts, and like coolies, we climb. Our designated home is in a slight depression in the ridge that forms the southern cliff edge. Contained by a rock-wall perimeter, the site has three picnic tables and two outhouses. We aim our tents into the wind and weight every corner with rocks. On the islands as well as the sea, the wind dominates, deals the day's plan, forms shelter in the lee, and wreaks danger to windward. It sweeps this dry island, sculpts the grasses of the meadows, and supports the hovering peregrine. It is no place to leave a dome tent unweighted.

Dinner will have to wait. Hungry as we are, the island has to be appreciated. Looking back over the meadow, past the Anacapa lighthouse and its twenty-four-hour foghorn, the mainland hills are blue in the distance, the channel flecked with whitecaps—most

noticeably a mile off our island where we had experienced the biggest waves and strongest wind. To the west behind the ridge, the light of sunset draws us out. We follow a path along the ridge which is edged with rocks on either side to keep us from straying onto the fragile grasses—a signal of a new and caring stewardship for this little island.

Leaning into a buffeting wind, our eyes follow the knifelike ridgelines of Anacapa's islets zigzagging toward the west. The sky is a pure yellow in the clean sunset air, the hills black in silhouette. Two ravens arc across the golden sky and drop below the cliff edge, to rise hovering almost within reach.

~~~

The following morning the wind I expected to be stilled rattles my tent. We brew coffee in the shelter of the outhouse—the only wind break we can find. Within the hour, Doug and Joanne herd us toward our kayaks, the lifeboatlike put-in, and the circumnavigation of Anacapa.

The same current we fought yesterday now scoots us around the eastern end of the island, through the picturesque arch that has become the symbol of the Channel Islands. Bathed in sun, rimmed by a filigree of pelicans, the arch resembles a natural, if slouching, Arc de Triomphe, standing free of the island among a number of smaller sea stacks and offshore reefs. Pelicans, cormorants, and gulls rise in complaint as we paddle under the arch and enter the quieter water on the south shore of the island.

It is as if the weather god flipped a switch—no wind. For twenty-four hours we have been leaning into the wind, cranking our voices up a notch just to be heard. Now it is so quiet we listen in awe. One by one we begin to strip off some layers of clothing, the heat of the sun now full force.

As my kayak drifts among the floating kelp, I drag my hand in the remarkably clear water. Far below, a brilliant flash of red-gold sparks my curiosity. Doug

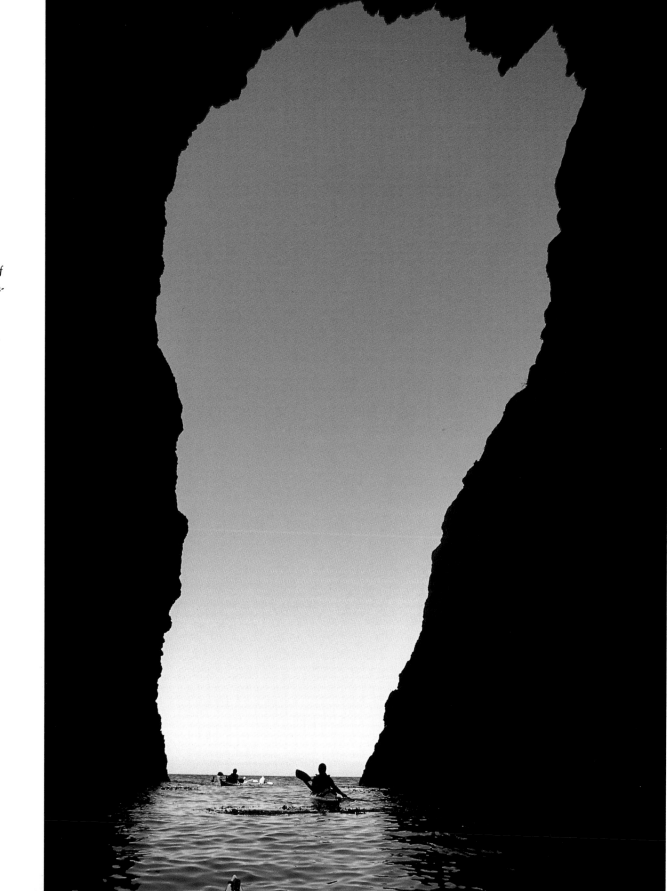

♦

Anacapa's north
coast has caves of
Hollywood dimen-
sions—so big,
all of us fit.

thinks it can only be a garibaldi—a rockfish the color of a California poppy. I follow its movements through the kelp forest until it blurs from sight.

Secretly I'm hoping a sea lion will pass beneath me; instead the next critter is a human, a diver no doubt after the garibaldi. Ahead, the diveboat that brought the diver lies at anchor. We had seen the craft that morning, bucking into the same conditions we paddled through yesterday. It must have over twenty scuba divers aboard. Safe behind Anacapa, the black-and-blue-garbed divers flop happily into the sea.

We paddle past their stares. One diver asks if we had paddled over, and we nod—John Wayne could not have done it better. I can't help but think of the Aleuts, who made the crossing in half the time.

In a brief and unusual period of California history, the Aleuts of the Aleutian Islands once hunted off the Channel Islands. Beginning in 1807 with an agreement between the Russian-American Company's Alexander Andreivich Baranov and one Joseph O'Cain of Boston, Aleut hunters with their sea kayaks—baidarkas as the Russians called them—were loaded aboard O'Cain's ships and brought 1,700 miles south from Alaska to hunt the sea otter.

Never had the hunters seen so many otters, defenseless against the numbers of men, the small swift kayaks, and the barbed bone lances. In the ensuing years, the ships of Boston would mother fleets of Aleut kayakers to hunt from Trinidad, which was near the present-day border of California and Oregon, to the Baja California peninsula. It was a headlong slaughter. There was no thought of conservation. And there is no record of the Aleuts who were conscripts at best—almost no mention of them at all. One of the few European comments about the Aleut hunters states that they took to the hunt "like the eager dog at the sight of game." In three years, 1809 through 1811, for example, over 8,000 sea otters were taken within San Francisco Bay alone, by fleets of over 140 sea kayaks.

Today, there are no sea otters at Anacapa. No one knows when the last one was killed—most likely around 1900. The Monterey sea otter community, the only local group to survive the hunt, is stable and healthy, numbering 1,645 as of November 1989. In 1987, a translocation community of twenty sea otters was established on San Nicolas Island, forty-four miles due south of Anacapa. Although it is too early to tell whether these otters will survive, it is the beginning of the sea otter's return to the protective kelp beds of the Channel Islands.

~~~

Paddling at an unhurried pace, we continue our circumpaddle, we are tailed by harbor seals instead of otters, and flying fish break the surface off our bows. Rounding the western tip of Anacapa, we expect to encounter the wind but are surprised instead by light air and a subdued sea. Doug is excited as he dons his helmet; we should have safe access to the cave-riddled northern coast.

The helmet is worn to cushion your head in case you get, as Doug calls it, "squeezed" against the roof of a cave by an invading wave. I strap the helmet provided by Southwinds Sports to my head, with appreciation. It's one thing to paddle into a dark cave beneath the weight of a rock and lava ceiling. But to float to the top of a marine cave and be pressed there like some cartoon character—this is the stuff of nightmares.

We paddle through the afternoon from cave to cave. Some are fractures with long, narrow entries; others are big enough to moor a sailboat in. There are tunnels and chambers, bends and turns in complete darkness. Others are like grottos painted with the colors of the sea. At each entrance, we watch the wave patterns and edge in one at a time. We move slowly, watching for hidden reefs and the sudden appearance of cave-dwelling cormorants. Doug goes first and Joanne takes up the rear, as we poke in and out of the underpinnings of Anacapa.

Doug and Joanne pause beneath a majestic cliff

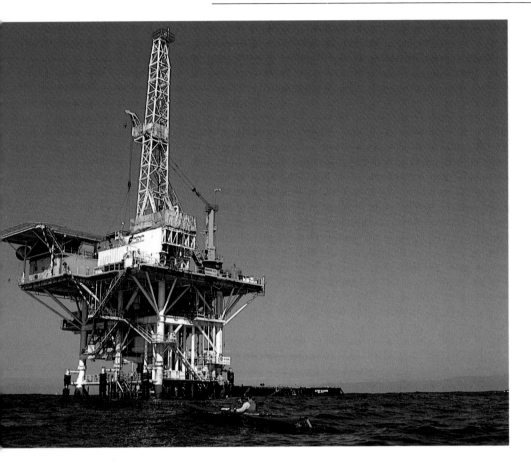

river of seawater. At times the passage is too cramped to paddle and I fend off the walls of what appears to be more like a mine shaft than a cave. Ahead, Richard is in white water. The waves that had passed ahead of him now rebound from the side chambers in a vision that would make Indïana Jones wince. A moment later I am caught in waves coming from three sides; my kayak rises and I automatically duck my head. I look up and realize I've passed through the corridor and into a grand chamber. I sweep to the left and wait as Joanne comes busting through, wide-eyed. One by one, we gather in a space perhaps 100 feet across. A filtered and refracted light from the three passages to the outside illuminates mosquelike vaulted ceilings tiled in lavender algae and rimmed by pale-green anemones and purple sea urchins. It is as wonderful a world as I've ever seen—a kayakers-only paradise. I linger until claustrophobia gets to me, and then I squeeze out into the soft light of the late afternoon.

We finish our long day of exploring, experiencing some of the most difficult and enchanting sea kayaking of our lives, conscious of the impact we have had on these beleaguered islands. Wilderness such as Cathedral Cave is an eroding entity in California, existing only in the inaccessible. Our kayaks are so suited to exploring the hidden parts of the coast. And yet it is sometimes difficult to accept our presence here.

We continually surprise an already weary wildlife on our return to camp. Doug cautions me from paddling too close to shore because there are sea lions around the next stack, and I change course without question. I'd like to think the self-actualizing nature of our sport creates an affinity with and an understanding of the wild places we explore. Although it is naive to think wisdom comes with the kayak and paddle, as our kayaking community grows we must honor and protect the rights of those living things we come in contact with.

Again we hoist the boats and take the hike back to camp in time for sunset. We will be gone in the morning.

Offshore oil rig "Gina" marks the route to Anacapa, a symbol of our precarious dependence on oil and the 1969 oil-well blowout that polluted the Santa Barbara channel.

rising about 200 feet. Past the kelp beds at its base a small opening is visible, protected by a perimeter of rocks and reefs. Doug pulls us together and explains: "This is what we call Cathedral Cave. You start by skirting the rocks, and once inside you follow me through a narrow corridor that opens to a set of chambers beneath the mass of the headland. There are three exits over on the other side of the point—all in safe water. Ready?"

One glance back past the rocks at a Maxfield Parrish scene of brilliant sun on alabaster sea stacks rising from an ultramarine sea and then I ride a mild swell into the darkness. Mayhem—my eyes dilating, I strain to see my surroundings, floating on a surging

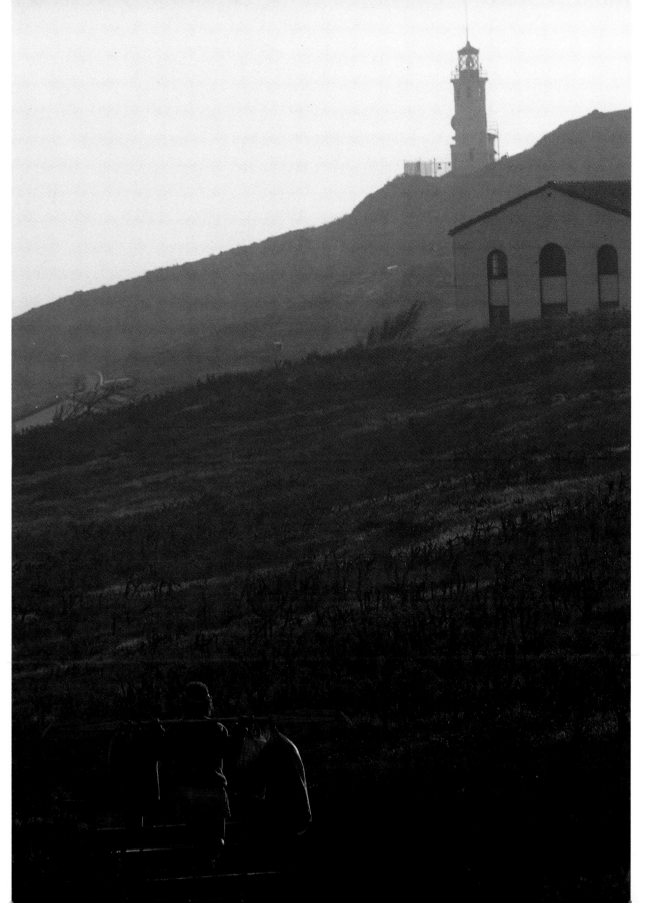

◆

On Anacapa
Island, Joanne
Turner walks with
the wind along the
now-familiar trail
from camp to
kayaks. The
Anacapa light-
house blinks in
the distance.

THE TRANSLUCENT SEA

♦

Baja and the Sea of Cortez

Everything concerning Baja California is of
such little importance that it is hardly worth
the trouble to take a pen and write about it.
Of poor shrubs, useless thorn bushes and bare
rocks, of miles of sand without water and
wood . . . what shall I or can I report?
—Johann Jakob Baeger, S.J., 1772

Stripped hills, cold volcano, stone and hot
wind under all that splendor, drought, the
taste of dust, and a pepper tree in the midst of
desert like a petrified fountain!
—Octavio Paz, 1963

BY MID-NOVEMBER, the first winter storms strike across
western Wyoming with freezing, sidecut winds and heavy
snow. The Seattle papers usually carry a wire-service

*Left: The other-
worldly form of a
pitaya dulce cactus
frames the desert
coastline of Baja
California and
the Sea of Cortez
in December
morning light.*

131

Mulegé

Punta Concepción

GULF OF CALIFORNIA

(Sea of Cortez)

Punta Colorado

Punta Santa Teresa

Bahía Concepción

Punta Púlpito

*San
Basilio
Bay*

Punta San Basilio

—*Caleta de San Juanico*
(San Juanico Cove)

BAJA CALIFORNIA DEL SUR

MEXICO

1

· THE TRANSLUCENT SEA ·

BAJA AND THE SEA OF CORTEZ

N

Loreto

piece telling which cities were hardest hit. I always read this first winter report to see whether it mentions Lander, Wyoming. For Lander is the home of Charles Fiala, former acting director of the National Outdoor Leadership School, my onetime roommate, and the friend who introduced me to both sea kayaking and Baja California. It usually takes one good storm, maybe two, to hit Lander before Charley digs himself out, calls me, and we begin planning our sometimes annual rendezvous south of the border.

We toss around dates and people: Standish from San Francisco, Chris Johnson out of Ketchum. Sarah's finals are over on the tenth, Fran has a commitment on March 2. Dracos and Patty can put us up in San Diego. Charley suggests that we take the "northern route," a classic paddle along the east coast of Baja. We set a date for mid-February, and assign group gear among those who are coming. Now we can accept winter's worst with the anticipation of remote coasts and guaranteed sun.

About twenty-five million years ago, Baja California slowly began to separate from the Mexican mainland. At a rate geologists estimate to be an inch a year, the entire land mass has traveled 450 miles to the north and west, causing the Gulf of California to form behind it. This intervening body of water, once called the Sea of Cortez, insulated the plant and animal populations, the indigenous people, and Father Johann Jakob Baeger for that matter, on a remnant of land 800 miles long and not more than 100 miles wide.

Baja is a volcanic landscape, the color of ochre and rust, the composition of sediment, ash, and lava. Beneath its overburden of volcanic soils lie ancient sea beds, fossilized rhododendrons, tropical vegetation, even twenty-ton duck-billed dinosaurs. Man has only scratched the surface—at Tijuana, La Paz, and Cabo San Lucas. The rest of the land is thinly settled, isolated, and quixotic beneath clear skies, flanked by warm seas, strewn with mountains, mesas, arroyos, and plains.

Our two-car caravan is 500 miles south of Tijuana on Highway 1, the only road that runs the length of the Baja peninsula. The guaranteed sun we had yearned for shimmers off the two-lane blacktop. Oncoming vehicles, miles distant across the flat landscape called the Vizcaino Desert, are dissolved into caricature in the heat, then loom closer, solidify, and pass with a roar.

The entire interior of our car is coated with a fine dust, the air we breathe is hot, and our consumption of liquids is constant. By mid-afternoon we turn east, the highway curving around streams of red, geologically recent lava flows. We pass mute cinder cones and then the road, flanked by dented and twisted guardrails, drops with a twelve-percent grade to the relative cool of the coast.

The first sight of the Sea of Cortez rivets road-weary minds—an intense blue sea, streaked with whitecaps in stark contrast to the dry land. We sidle along the water's edge, heading south past Santa

Mulegé, an oasis of palms crowned by a 300-year-old prison, is our last stop for groceries and water before our put-in.

133

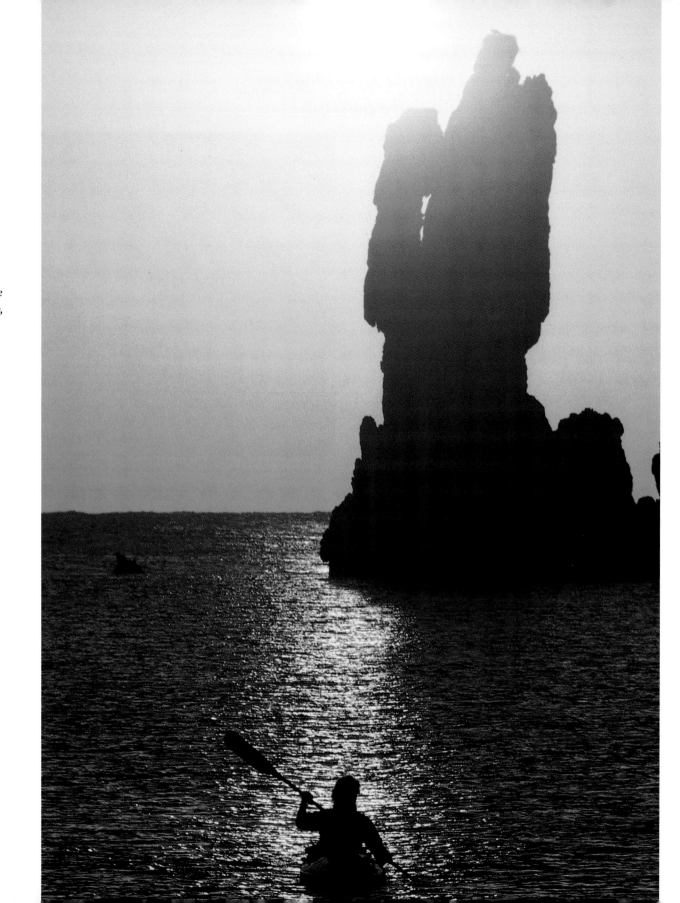

◆

Silhouetted in the sun, a monumental sea stack, home of an osprey family, overshadows a sea kayaker in San Juanico Cove.

Rosalía's ancient, still-active copper mines, past the many roadside shrines commemorating bad luck on the narrow, seacliff road. Within an hour, our dusty automobiles pull into the remarkably tropical town of Mulegé, a seventeenth-century Spanish settlement sited along a palm-lined river. Charley guides us to a *mercado* to obtain the essentials of a true Baja expedition: limes, small cans of Heredez hot sauce, potent garlic and onions, fresh tortillas, and water—gallons of water.

Our put-in is a small mangroved bay just south of town, which is overrun each year with an increasing number of RVs. Amidst the satellite dishes and the open shelters with palm-frond roofs, we unload across the beach, sorting gear—each of us focusing on our individual load plans. After the last items are coerced behind seats or strapped on top of our decks, we gather to look at the route.

With the point of his knife, Charley traces our route on the old nautical chart of the Golfo de California from the USS *Narragansett* surveys of 1873 and 1875. The blade crosses three miles of open water from Mulegé to Punta Concepción and then edges south down the east side of a long, roadless peninsula. Cutting into places Charley has visited and named during his years as director of the National Outdoor Leadership School's (NOLS) Baja branch, he describes the "aquarium," "lobster cove," and "plant place." For seventy miles, we will follow the route pioneered by the school over twenty years ago when "Tap" Tappley first brought the beamy Folbots south from Lander. Charley's rising excitement is infectious; we've got fourteen days to take our time, staying longer at the magic camps, moving when the weather allows.

Weather plays a background theme on every Baja trip. The gulf is a windy place, with wind enough to hold experienced kayakers in camp for days; hence the built-in extra time in our schedule. This morning it's calm and cloudless, which doesn't amount to a hill of frijoles anywhere along this coast. In winter, the wind blows from the north without clouds and without warning. Our policy will be to follow NOLS's long-established pre-dawn starts, to paddle through the calm early hours into the glorious sunrise until wind or destination takes us ashore. Charley closes his knife with a snap. We turn to our boats and the last bit of packing; we're now down to the delicate use of full body weight to close hatches.

A Baja trip means a full boat: lots of toys for fishing, snorkeling, and pictures. The unfamiliar environment demands a library of books on birds, plants, fish, and the stars. Two weeks of food becomes a thirty-five-pound duffle bag. Charley had said on our first trip many years ago, "If you don't get a wetsuit, you don't go. It's fifty percent of the trip." Ever since, I've packed a wetsuit top, weight belt, mask, snorkel, booties, and fins—all but the tanks and regulator. Special Baja items include a sun tarp, a grill, clothes for the chill of evening, and a goodly supply of aloe vera for sunburn. On top of all that, five gallons of water are needed—enough for six to eight hot days. We drag our boats to the cool waters of the Bahía de Concepción. My kayak is so heavy it has a momentum of its own, as I point east toward the slow mountainous rise of Punta Concepción.

From previous trips comes the memory of our first camp, "the aquarium," seven miles distant. Just over the raised, flat headland that protects the landing lies a white sand beach. White sand blending to the color of the sea. I have been thinking of this one beach ever since Charley's call, imagining the infinite gradations of the sea's color from the palest lime stretching to an infinite series of deepening greens and azures and on to blues, my torso plunging into the wet world, fish scattering in silver surprise. John Steinbeck wrote about the Sea of Cortez in 1941:

> The sea here swarms with life, and probably the ocean bed is equally rich. Microscopically, the water is crowded with plankton. This is the tuna water-life water. It is complete from plankton

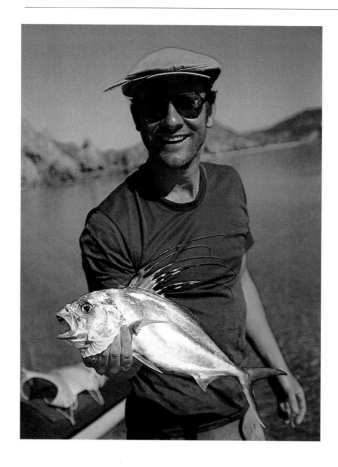

A rooster fish meets the food chain in the form of Charley Fiala.

Far right: Kayakers scud before the wind at five-plus knots. The peaks of the Sierra de la Giganta mountains pass in the distance.

Twenty feet below is a series of long lava fingers running outward from the beach. Between them are lanes of sand, white carpets where only the hunters swim. I look for the rays—stingrays—vague diamond shapes concealed there.

In the dim blue distance, my vivid imagination conjures sharks. But they are sharks, gliding effortlessly on the edge of my vision. As they come closer, I realize with relief that they are only three or four feet long. Just as elegant and sleek as their parents, the trio of sharks with eerie eyes and a predator's urgency swim past, perhaps searching for the cabrilla, a delicate white fish Charley prefers for our favorite Baja appetizer ceviche— raw cabrilla marinated in lime juice, garlic, and salsa. I return to the surface, grab a deep breath, and instinctively submerge to search them out again—they are gone. Getting chilled and hungry, I swim back through the reef to our wind-protected cove and a welcome first night's dinner: ceviche, lobster, beans and rice, cornbread, coffee, and walnut pie.

In Baja, rain falls as if by lottery. One place may go for a year without a drop, while a neighboring valley is green with excess. But excess seldom means more than five inches a year—all in two or three torrential downpours. Baja is a land of stress and adaptation, as Joseph Wood Krutch describes in his book *Baja California and the Geography of Hope:*

> *In desert country everything from the color of a mouse or the shape of a leaf up to the largest features of the mountains themselves is more likely than not to have the same explanation: dryness. So far as living things go, all this adds up to what even an ecologist may so far forget himself as to call an "unfavorable environment." But like all such pronouncements this one doesn't mean much unless we ask "unfavorable for what and for whom?"*

to gray porpoises. . . . There was food everywhere. Everything ate everything else with a furious exuberance.

Now I hover just beneath the surface, tossed by the swell sweeping in above me. My body is pulled toward the reef, then released as the wave passes in a swirl of sunlit bubbles. The fins give me a speed so unlike swimming that I squirrel around the lagoon in bursts of joy. In the clefts and pockets of the reef, tiny fish watch as if curious, their little mouths working, their fins stabilizing iridescent bodies suspended in a translucent sea.

Beyond the reef, I launch out over a sea cliff.

At every new landing, once we've set up camp and gone for a welcome swim, the arroyo beckons. As a rule,

our camps are on a beach formed by the outwash of the dry creek beds, or arroyos, that cut through the coastline to the sea. The curiosity of what lies up the arroyo begins with what at first appears to be a road—a country lane drawing me past giant cardon cacti. But it is actually a meticulously neat streambed curving back and forth between steep, matching hillsides.

When it rains, a hard-driving rain, this quiet canyon path is transformed into a chocolate-colored, boulder-carrying, flood-stage river. In the subsiding violence, sand sloughing from the hillsides renews the pathway and fills the scoured channel with another neat, flat layer.

On the hillsides stand cacti swollen from the rain: fat little barrel cacti, multiarmed hedgehog cacti, and the galloping cactus, the cholla, whose living limbs radiate out from a long-dead root stalk. There are trees and shrubs here that have their own methods of desert survival: the creosote bush has varnished leaves to retard evaporation, the *torote* or elephant tree limits its leaves to tiny, evergreen leaflets in complete disproportion to its thigh-sized limbs. Visually dominant on the hillside is the *palo blanco*, perhaps the most beautiful tree in Baja, with its tall, slender, white limbs that reflect heat and its paper-thin leaves that minimize moisture loss. I decide to have lunch in the half-shade of a *palo blanco*: raisins, cheddar cheese, and water.

The best lesson of the arroyo can be gained by sitting in one spot. Within minutes, life activities resume that your exploring had suspended: a grey lizard tongues by, butterflies flit, a Costas hummingbird hovers above my head and then races off on supersonic wings. I hear a breeze work up the arroyo from the sea, carrying the staccato sound of an unseen woodpecker. Not much else moves at noon in heat that is near eighty degrees. The energy of the arroyo lies dormant, to be heard tonight in quick movements and the workings of little jaws.

Our traveling days begin ninety minutes before sunrise, with Charley shaking tents. Like well-oiled

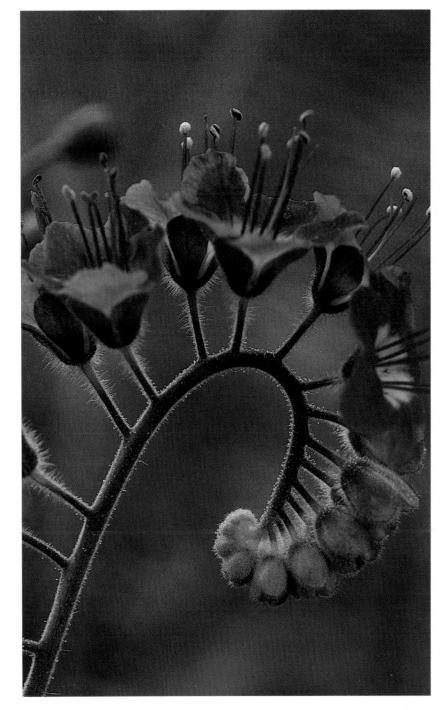

machines, we bump and clang in the darkness, filling dry bags and lugging them boatward in an attempt to beat the sun. Periodically, one of us stops to feel for the wind—alert to the first breath that may mean a wind delay. But as the light of the sun turns the Sea of Cortez a brilliant orange, we slide our kayaks into the still water, adjust our paddles, and take the first strokes into a calm day.

Our third travel day, we stay in a loose formation throughout the morning, paddling through the rising heat. On our left, the Gulf of California plays host to passing porpoises and flights of pelicans, and the shore reveals the volcanic layering of red lava and white ash.

Our water supply has dwindled and water sources along the way are few. We take advantage of a passing sloop, manned by winter refugees from Vancouver, British Columbia, who gladly top off our jugs.

There are few travelers along this coast. Offshore, sailboats sometimes mark the horizon, as do the rusty shrimpers and the occasional power yacht. Due to the prevailing north wind, all the kayakers paddle south. There must be at least ten guide services joining NOLS on this route, shepherding groups of kayakers, others at times sharing our bay without crowding. This year there are more people than in years past, but a shared environmental responsibility continues to maintain this coast's wild character.

By noon, we pass Junkyard Beach, our eventual take-out and end of trip. This somber note dwells in our minds, as our arms automatically carve the paddles through the water. A flight of pelicans glides by down-wind, inches off the sea's surface. One by one, we notice and follow their movements with fascination.

On the Baja trip, the brown pelican is our constant, ever-entertaining neighbor. These large seabirds travel low on the water, drafting the bird ahead—beak to tail feather. They contour the flat swell much as land birds do a thermal, timing short bursts of wing thrusts in relation to the rise of the wave. They gain four to six feet, then glide for all they're worth until their wingtips skim the swell. We watch them go, disappearing around the headland into San Juanico Cove, as much their favorite campsite as ours.

San Juanico is a large, unusually beautiful cove on the southern end of San Basilio Bay. Well protected by high headlands, at its center is a cluster of towering sea stacks crowned by osprey nests. Overhead, magnificent frigatebirds circle, and beyond, in a series of scalloped coves, the pelicans have found a school of *sardinas.* We paddle happily toward the beach, anticipating an extended swim and the simple pleasure of watching the birds.

This is our final camp. Our remaining days are spent snorkeling amidst the diving pelicans, feasting on Charley's daily catch, and listening to the osprey's calls piercing the distance. Lying on the beach, I can't help thinking that someday there's going to be a road into this area—a nagging thought on our last afternoon. The osprey calls again, greeting her mate as he glides across the sky. Together we watch his approach, flare, and landing on the nest.

Suddenly at the shoreline, the water is alive with movement—we stare dumbfounded as Charley sprints to the water's edge and begins scooping fish after fish in our direction. Mullet are beaching themselves to avoid a predator. With Charley's added assistance, they fly through the air, crashing into the bushes to become our dinner instead. We retrieve a bounty of quivering sixteen- to twenty-inch-long fish doomed to the cutting board, the garlic, and limes. While the fish marinates, we settle back, staring out across the tranquil bay.

As this trip to Baja ends, I am amazed that annually we go through the trouble, risking our necks on the roads, and braving Montezuma's revenge, scorpion bites, and the *federales,* just to spend a few quiet days like these. There is an exotic quality to this coast, where life is so different and so precious, that keeps us returning, repeating the same route south of Mulegé, year after year.

MANGROVE MAÑANA

La Manzanilla

THE CONSTANT SOUND is a dry rasping of palm fronds, the thatch roof of a substantial though neglected *palapa* standing in the wind. The intermittent sound is the surf along the beach, zippering from right to left, sometimes coming ashore with so little force it fails to break, like a heart skipping a beat. I stop and listen through the sudden silence until the rhythmic pattern begins again. In time the wave sequence builds to a height somewhere approaching three feet, and the beach rings with the shrill squeals and laughter of tumbling children.

Occasionally I hear another sound, overhead, muted, and at first unidentifiable—a tracery of big, urgent wing beats passing north to south. It is the sound of an anhinga, a giant cormorantlike bird, flying low and fast for the safety of the mangroves. Before I open my eyes the sound is gone, blended into the simple song of a La Manzanilla afternoon.

Our *palapa* is a simple beach structure common along both coasts of Mexico, made of forked tree-limb uprights that support a beam and thatch roof. It is ideal

Left: Sleepy La Manzanilla awakens, and townspeople come to barter and buy the fishermen's catch.

143

Puerto Vallarta

JALISCO

MEXICO

200

Bahía Tenacatita ● La Manzanilla

● Punta Tamarinda

Cabeza de Navidad — ● Melaqué

Bahía Navidad

Manzanillo

· MANGROVE MAÑANA ·

LA MANZANILLA

because it provides shade and is open to the cool breezes of the seashore. Ours is without walls, the only furniture a kitchen table, shelves for supplies, various chairs and campstools, a fence to keep out the animals, and the hammock I now occupy.

A body moves past me. Julie Stimson, the assistant guide, is heading for the beach. Our people must be back—sea kayaking Christmas vacationers bent on what can only be termed relentless fun. I prop myself up in the hammock and watch the approach of the kayaks. Julie wades into the sea, poised with a line to hook on the stern of the first beachbound double in case the kayak begins to broach. The others in singles and doubles wait offshore. One by one the boats come through the surf, legs emerge, dry bags are piled on the beach, and the boats are hiked up past my hammock, past the *palapa*, to be bedded down near our tents.

The people in the group are from Seattle or Anchorage, their once winter-white exteriors now brown in the twenty-degree-latitude sun, their parched interiors intent on the coolers, liquids, fruit juice, and beer.

I suppose I should get up. Soon it will be time for dinner: fresh tamales, a shrimp-and-coconut soup, a dorado fish with a cilantro hot sauce, and, with the help of a battery-operated ice crusher, piña coladas. I plant my feet on either side of the hammock and lever up, using reserves of energy saved up over the afternoon. Heading for the tent and a change of clothes to insulate me from the cool of the evening and the dusk assault of mosquitoes, I take a zigzag path to avoid being hit by the head-crushing coconuts that periodically thud into the sand.

La Manzanilla is a town that is not included in the indexes of the Mexico guidebooks, nor does it show up on detailed maps. It is a town on the edge of the Pacific Ocean, 200 kilometers south of Puerto Vallarta and 100 kilometers north of Manzanillo. A small road sign along the coastal highway signals its existence, and a dirt road leads from the blacktop three kilometers west

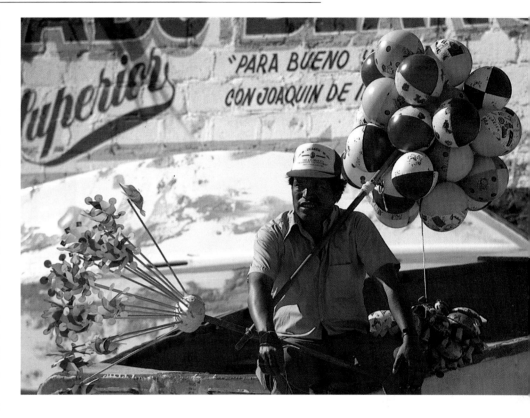

to its small grid of dusty streets—home to about 600 people. They live in small brick and adobe houses, run a few substantial *mercados*, and get baptized, married, and mourned at a new, jarringly modern Catholic church. A few families with haciendas on the beach have opened restaurants. But aside from the church and the few new pickup trucks baking in the sun, La Manzanilla has the look of a miniature 1920s banana republic, persisting for generations without much attention from the outside world.

Not that we are the answer to their prayers. Fame, fortune, and tourists may come to La Manzanilla, but not through us. We are incidental visitors, curiosities with kayaks, shopping for food in the *mercado*, buying fish from the *pangas* pulled up on the beach. We are a type the townspeople will probably never see again

Patricio Salestino, balloon vendor, rests between sales on the beach at Melaqué, Bahía de Navidad.

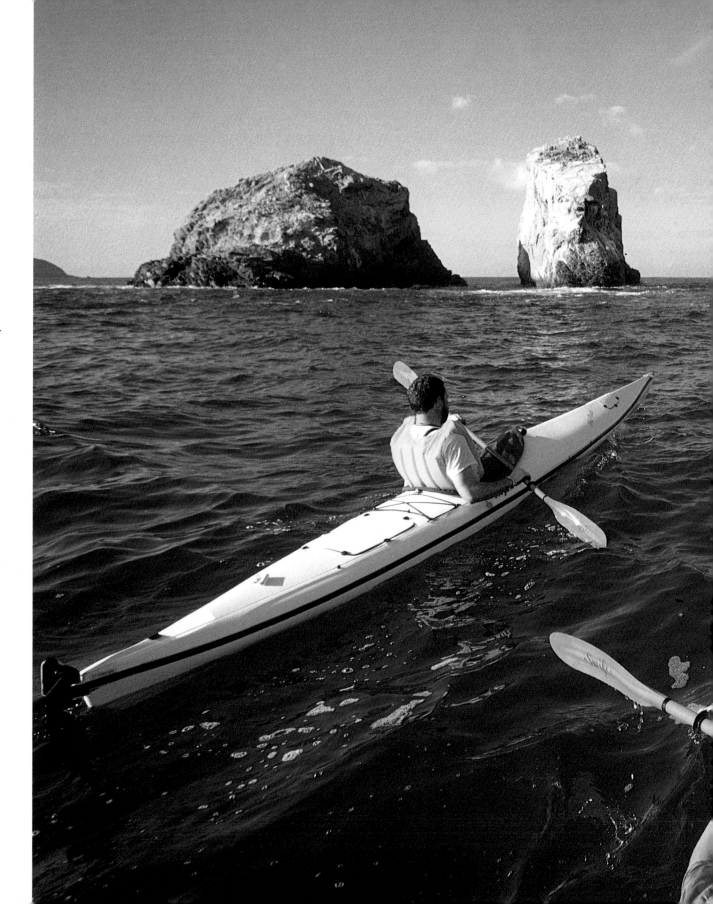

"The Churches,"
a set of small sea
stacks, challenge
kayakers with their
narrow channels
and sea surges off
La Manzanilla.

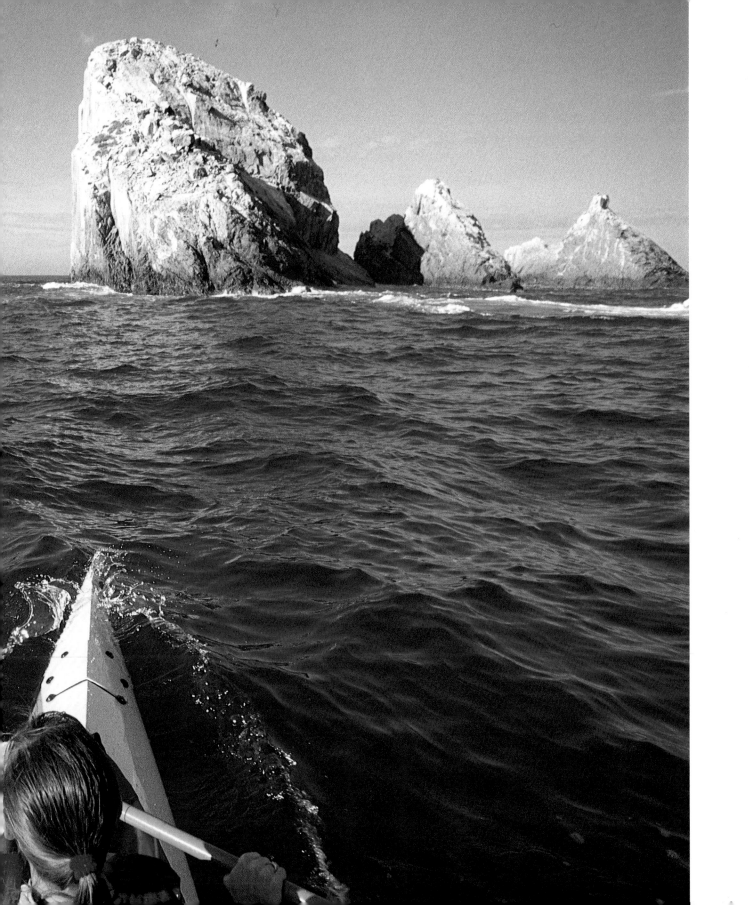

◆

Sarah Shannon and a land iguana share a perfect beach known as Mismaloya.

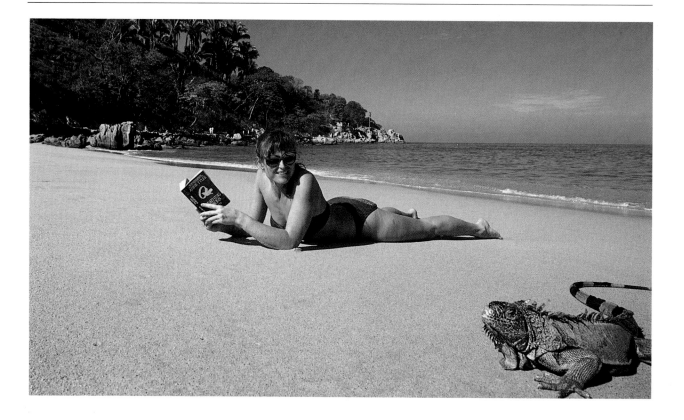

when and if the long white beach fills in with hotels, golf courses, and T-shirt stands.

Scott Roberge, head guide of Seattle-based Outback Expeditions, wants to know my opinion of the decision to come to La Manzanilla. He's got the question all kayak outfitters ask themselves: is it a successful idea? This is Outback's first group to visit La Manzanilla after two years of waiting for Mexican licensing and bureaucrats, promotion, and logistics. I reply that it's perfect, in an unusual, on-the-edge-of-wilderness way.

～～

Nine days ago we arrived at Puerto Vallarta, one of Mexico's many "gold coasts." Scott collected us from our afternoon flights, and we piled into a van and headed south past the gigantic tourist hotels, the old town,

and the slums. I retreated to the back of the van, and from my prone position atop a ton of gear bags I listened to snatches of get-acquainted conversation, as my inverted view changed from highrises and telephone wires to a canopy of second-growth jungle and starlight.

By the time we arrived at base camp we had placed names with faces, hometowns, and professions: an architect, a federal office worker, a teacher, a clothes designer for Eddie Bauer, a stockbroker, and my friend Sarah, a Ph.D. candidate in nursing ethics. We sorted out our bags, and using flashlights found our tents. Paul, the Anchorage stockbroker, suggested a night swim, and the unpacking became a search for bathing suits. Out of the shadows we came, laughing into the surf.

The water was warmer than the night. Waves approached in the darkness, catching us by surprise, breaking with a phosphorescent glow. Along the shore, few signs of man rimmed the bay, called Bahía Tenacatita. Just two clusters of light, an RV enclave and a hotel complex, defined the northern curve. Above them, the North Star and the Great Bear were low on the hills. To the south, the town slumbered under a few incongruously bright mercury vapor lights.

Dawn revealed a dry, tropical landscape of volcanic hills beneath grey-green vegetation. Outcrops of rock punctuated the coast. A few rugged islands known as "the Churches" lay near the mouth of the crescent-shaped bay, and a mangrove swamp nestled behind us, penetrating inland.

For a few days, we acclimatized to the hot, breezy, humid world of the beach and the random events of a town swelling with the arrival of local Guadalajara Christmas vacationers. We learned about kayaks, paddling techniques, beach landings, and self-rescue—each day paddling across Bahía Tenacatita. Taking snorkles and a sun tarp, we visited remote palm-fringed beaches, read and talked, spread corn tortillas with ripe avocados, white fish, and hot sauce, and cooled off with Mexican beer and triple-sweet Mexican soda pop. We relaxed and warmed to an exotic land on the edge of the Pacific.

The noise of a motorcycle, one of those nasty three-wheeled ORVs overloaded with three, maybe four small children, interrupts my thoughts as it blasts down the beach. Trash blows past my tent on the fresh afternoon breeze. I rummage through my bag for a fresh shirt, thinking what a tarnished heaven La Manzanilla is— a paradise on the edge of discovery.

The palapa has become a hub of special experiences like the hidden facets of an uncut gem. Each venture into the sunlight is totally different, a crossing into other worlds—from little girls in crisp white confirmation dresses who shyly bid us welcome, to an underwater wilderness, clear, colorful, and quiet beneath the sea.

Beyond the hammock lie the sweep and the occasional solitude of the four-mile beach. But one unsuspected world, unknown for three days though only 200 feet from the palapa, would prove to be the finest facet of them all. Sarah remembers: "The moment that stands out for me was discovering the swamp, the mangroves, parrots flying overhead . . . coming around that one corner and seeing the white ibis. I've gone past that page in the bird book and seen that bird a thousand times, but never in the wild."

Sarah and I first paddle the mangrove swamp at dawn on the third morning, going in where the mangrove trees jut toward the sea and neatly hide a narrow surge channel. The waxy-green mangrove leaves, a visual and physical barrier from camp, part and we enter into a series of surprisingly large lakes. The foliage of the rounded mangrove trees hangs over the water; there is no visible bank, no high ground, just a continuous wall of vegetation supported by radial fans of mahogany-red roots that disappear into the turbid, coffee-colored water. By guesswork and the recent signs of Scott and his assistants' machetes—they had cleared some of the routes that had grown impassable—we wind our way deeper into the swamp following tunnel-like passages that take us through an environment different from any we have ever seen.

Mangrove swamps are a belittled biome. The rich foliage of the mangrove tree itself makes it look like your basic tree, but a closer inspection reveals that its roots are in water, saline to fresh, in the shallow lagoons that buffer much of the subtropical to tropical coastlines of the world. These are difficult environments for man, and despite the fact that they provide habitat and sanctuary to numerous species of plant, animal, bird, and fish, mangroves are routinely destroyed with righteous abandon. But this mangrove swamp on the outskirts of La Manzanilla percolates along in good health without much hindrance from the townspeople.

On our first paddle, Sarah and I explore until we end within earshot of the highway. En route we see

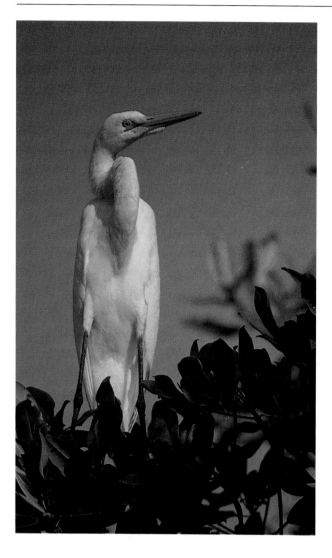

◆

*A great white
heron perches in
the crown of a
mangrove tree
moments before
its shy flight.*

*Far right: In
mangroves, a
ready ear and a
quick eye discover
hidden life in the
shade and foliage.*

That morning we begin a fascination with the mangrove that in time is shared by all in our group. Once Scott has taken the group through, each day at dawn or dusk a couple of kayakers put in on the channel and disappear through the canopy, returning with stories of flocks of jabbering parrots, the rare sight of a cayman (a tropical American crocodilian), and a roost tree filled with white egrets. On our final evening in La Manzanilla, Sarah catches me at the tent and convinces me we should take a last paddle through the mangrove together. Dinner can wait.

We check with Scott and he agrees to save us a meal. We grab a couple of Wind Dancers and slide them into the skin-temperature water. As our kayaks clear the entry foliage, a pair of black-crowned night herons leaps into the sky, while unseen others sidestep deeper into the jungle of limbs and leaves. As we paddle slowly along the edge of the lake, our ears listen for life just within the canopy, as our eyes watch the far mangrove tops for the long necks and tapered bodies of the many fishing birds home from the sea. In the early evening, as the last direct sun hits the far shore, the swamp is noisy with the classic tropical calls of the wild.

We have improved our ability to spot the various birds perched in the dense branches and root structures, and through our repeated paddles into the swamp, we have learned where most of them congregate. We speed up at times, then drift to a crawl as we pass through a constricted section of overhanging vegetation, just to avoid disturbing the cormorants and ibises on their perches. The water is perfectly still, mirror-imaging the bulging crowns of the mangrove trees in the warm light of sunset. I have a 300-mm telephoto lens on my camera and am waiting for a chance opportunity, when we round a bend and flush a great white heron with a seventy-inch wingspan—the largest bird in residence.

The heron flies down the channel, and just as it turns out of sight it begins to flare, a sure sign that it has landed. We gather speed and then drift, ruddering

more exotic birds than either of us has ever seen at any one time, short of in an aviary. Along with the anhinga, we manage to find a solitary black hawk, a snowy egret, great white herons, a little blue heron, numerous green herons, the tasseled black-crowned night heron, and white ibises. Though the *Golden Field Guide to the Birds of North America* says white ibises are not here, they are. We are ecstatic.

around the corner, our camera and binoculars ready. For the next ten minutes our boats close the sixty feet to the heron, neither Sarah nor I moving a muscle. My camera and lens become heavy but I dare not move. I shoot a few insurance shots at a distance, and the heron jumps at the clicks. I can feel Sarah just behind me, patient while I stalk the photograph. At fifteen feet, we are still moving with the current at about a foot a minute, when the great bird begins to show signs of anxiety. I shoot a set of pictures as it lifts and flies, again within the channel to another waterside perch. Quietly, we backpaddle and make our way in the gathering dusk.

As the day ends, flights of raucous parrots, bright green with red highlights, skim the treetops. Egrets in a white "V" follow the pattern of lakes highlighted in the afterglow of sunset. Pairs of ibises stare out at us from their haunts, and once, a roseate spoonbill voicing the end of the day circles and lands at its preferred night roost. Without speaking, we paddle steadily and carefully past them. In a strange truce, few fly as we progress. Our course is set on the site we've come to call the Christmas tree.

Scott had talked of it from his days of clearing paths into the mangrove. Some of our friends had found it in their evening forays. It is the night tree of the snowy egrets, an aged mangrove, nearly leafless, centered in a side lagoon that opens to the beach and a backdrop of setting sun behind palms. As we approach the opening, we both slow, and looking right go still. About 100 feet away is a white tree, our Christmas tree, decked with snowy egrets—so many they brighten the evening, silhouetted against the failing light. We drift past the clearing and the mangrove closes in again. I do not shoot a picture, technically impossible with what I have. Yet we are happy to leave the egrets to their gregarious evening, safe in their accustomed mangrove.

Satisfied with a final glimpse, we tuck our mental images safely away and turn toward the tarnished heaven of La Manzanilla.

◆

Left: The pleasure of a western shore—a warm evening, still air, and the setting sun along the Pacific coast of Mexico.

NOTES

◆

Oil to Ice: Prince William Sound (pp. 15-27)

The epigraph for this chapter was excerpted from an article in the *Anchorage Daily News* on the oil spill, August 5, 1989.

After decimation of the sea otter population, federal regulation was enacted when the 1911 North Pacific Fur Seal Convention established initial protection for the sea otter, and the sea otters rebounded to approximately 10,000 animals at the time of the 1989 spill. The Anchorage U.S. Fish and Wildlife Service count of otters killed and recovered in the spill is 1,016, per their report dated December 19, 1989. See Art Davidson's *In the Wake of the* Exxon Valdez (San Francisco: Sierra Club Books, 1989), p. 394.

John Muir's 1902 remark on the Chugach Range is from "The Pacific Coast Glaciers," a chapter in his book *The Harriman Alaska Expedition*, Vol. I. (New York: Doubleday, Page, 1902), p. 132.

Going Outside: Chichagof Island (pp. 29-39)

The Tlingit, pronounced roughly Clink-it, live throughout Southeast Alaska. They along with the mainland Haida are the northernmost indigenous groups of the Pacific Northwest Coast Indians living in Alaska. Hoonah, meaning "place where the north wind doesn't blow," is the only large Tlingit settlement remaining on Chichagof Island.

The Knife's Edge: The Queen Charlotte Islands (pp. 41-51)

George F. MacDonald's observation about the Haida world is from his book *Haida Monumental Art: The Villages of the Queen Charlotte Islands* (Vancouver: University of British Columbia Press, 1983), p. 3.

Orca: Johnstone Strait to Blackfish Sound (pp. 53-63)

Paul Spong's 1974 statement about the orca is from his article "The Whale Show" in a collection of readings, *Mind in the Waters*, assembled by Joan McIntyre, editor (New York: Charles Scribner and Sons, 1974), p. 173.

Hunting of orcas is discussed in Eric Hoyt, *ORCA: A Whale Called Killer* (Ontario: Camden East, 1984), p. 255. A study by U.S. veterinarian Mark Keyes in 1970 on captive orca whales in Puget Sound revealed that twenty-five percent of the whales sampled had bullet wounds.

Skana, the whale Paul Spong studied for so many years, died of an infection at the age of eighteen. A member of the K-23 pod, she was captured in Puget Sound at the age of five. For the rest of her life, she performed in captivity at the aquarium in Vancouver, British Columbia.

Paul Spong's research contributed to the awareness that orcas respond to sound more readily than to visual cues. He discovered this with Skana, and by the mid-1970s, the Johnstone Strait orcas were being entertained and observed listening to rock music, Paul Horn's flute, synthesized recreations, and recordings of the whales' own sounds.

Paul Spong's research has continued for twenty years on Hanson Island, where David Arcese's sea kayaking groups periodically visit. For more information on Spong's research, see Rex Weyler's *Song of the Whale* (Garden City, New York: Doubleday, 1986).

Research into whale sounds is an ongoing area of study. Some research indicates that whales "echolocate" to "see" under water. According to this research, by using rapid high- and low-frequency clicks, an orca can identify fish species, maintain spatial relations with the pod, and avoid obstacles. For additional information on orcas and whales in general, see McIntyre, *Mind in the Waters*.

Point of Contact: Nootka Sound (pp. 65-73)

The derivation of the name Yuquot is discussed in Hilary Stewart's book *The Adventures and Sufferings of John R. Jewitt, Captive of Maquinna* (Vancouver: Douglas & McIntyre, 1987), p. 14.

South Fork: The Skagit River Estuary (pp. 75-85)

My "Eternal Thermos" was so named for its opportune arrival at the side of my boat during an outing on the Skagit flood of 1979. A stainless steel, two-quart Thermos, it was unaccountably cast adrift upstream and still had warm coffee—black—in it.

· NOTES ·

The first wintering of snow geese in the Skagit River estuary is discussed in an unpublished paper by Larry Brewer dated 1976. Brewer was once the Skagit state game range manager, and introduced me to estuaries. He is now an environmental quality manager at the Institute for Wildlife Environmental Toxicology at Clemson University in Clemson, South Carolina.

Shi Shi: The Olympic Peninsula Seashore (pp. 87-95)

Glen Sims's song is titled "Go To Sea Once More." A tune reminiscent of "Greensleeves," it was known as a "forebitter"—a type of sea shanty sung off watch in the forward crew's quarters, or fo'c'sle, of sailing ships. This particular version was popular with the sailors of Liverpool and has no known author or date of origin. For information, see Stan Hugill's *Shanties from the Seven Seas* (New York: E. P. Dutton & Co., 1961), pp. 581-85.

The comment about the development of rogue waves in the ocean is from K. E. Lilly, Jr., *Marine Weather of Western Washington* (Seattle: Starpath Publications, 1983), p. 29.

Gunkholing: The Oregon and California Coasts (pp. 109-19)

A fine regional book that delves into the history of the area's backroads is Mike Hayden's *Exploring the North Coast* (San Francisco: Chronicle Books, 1982).

The *Coast Pilot* is a fascinating and invaluable source of coastal marine information, tables, charts, and photographs published by the U.S. Government to supplement the nautical charts. See *The United States Coast Pilot*, Vol. 7, *Pacific Coast: California, Oregon, Washington, and Hawaii*, 25th ed. (Washington, D.C.: National Ocean Service, 1989), p. 201.

Anacapa Crossing: The Santa Barbara Channel Islands (pp. 121-29)

A comprehensive source of information on Anacapa Island and the other channel islands is Karen James Dowty's *A Visitor's Guide: The California Channel Islands* (Ventura, Calif.: Seaquit Books, 1984).

The comment made about the enthusiasm of early Aleut sea otter hunters is from Adele Ogden, *The California Sea Otter Trade 1784-1848*, Volume 26, (Berkeley, Calif.: The University of California Publications, 1941), p. 13. This book offers the most detailed description of the sea otter trade of that time.

Data on sea otter harvests in the nineteenth century are from George B. Dyson, "An Illicit Alliance, the California Sea Otter Boom of 1803-1841," *Sea Kayaker* 4:1, 1987, p. 11. This article, as well as George Dyson's book *Baidarka* (Seattle: Alaska Northwest Books, 1986), provide an indepth look at the Aleuts and their sea kayaks and a historical account of their involvement in the California sea otter hunt. Another detailed account of the Aleuts can be found in the translation of Ivan Veniaminov's 1840 *Notes on the Islands of the Unalaska District*, translated by Lydia Black and R. H. Geoghegan and edited by Richard A. Pierce (Fairbanks: Limestone Press, University of Alaska History Department, 1984). Richard Batman's *The Outer Coast* (New York: Harcourt Brace Jovanovich, 1985) provides a good overview of the West Coast of North America through the era.

The Translucent Sea: Baja and the Sea of Cortez (pp. 131-41)

The epigraphs for this chapter are from: Johann Jakob Baeger, S.J., *Observations in Lower California*, 1772, translated by M. M. Brandenburg and Carl L. Baumann (Berkeley: University of California Press, 1952), p. 5; and Octavio Paz, "The Broken Jar," *The Selected Poems of Octavio Paz* (Bloomington: Indiana University Press, 1968), p. 165.

John Steinbeck's quote is from *Log from the Sea of Cortez* (New York: Penguin Books, 1986 [1941]), p. 54.

Joseph Wood Krutch's book, *Baja California and the Geography of Hope* (San Francisco: Sierra Club Books, 1967), p. 34.

ACCESS GUIDE

◆

A NOTE ON SAFETY AND ACCESS: The information in *The Hidden Coast* is not intended to provide instruction on safely paddling or leading any of the trips. For educational information, see books like John Dowd's *Sea Kayaking*. The listing below for degree of difficulty—beginner, intermediate, and expert—indicates a varied marine environment from safe to dangerous in average weather conditions.

Oil to Ice: Prince William Sound, Alaska (pp. 15-27)

LOCATION: 50 miles east-southeast of Anchorage, Alaska. Due west of Cordova.

SEASON: From May 15 to September 15. Best May 15 to June 1, for the fewest bugs and best bird-watching; July for best summer weather.

TRIP LENGTH: Prince William Sound calls for extended stays. From Whittier, it takes 1 week minimum to paddle to Harriman Fjord and back; 2 weeks is optimal for that area. Consider a shuttle to get you to Knight Island.

DEGREE OF DIFFICULTY: Beginner (with expert companions) to expert.

GETTING THERE/PUT-IN: By air to Anchorage. Charter air service on floats for remote drop-off by Ketchum Air, tel. (800)433-9114. To Whittier put-in, take Intercity Bus Lines, tel. (907)279-3221 for 50-mile trip to Portage, where the Alaska Railroad provides 6 daily trains to Whittier from May 15 to September 15 and 3 shuttles a week during the remaining year. Cordova has daily jet service to southeast Prince William Sound.

PUT-IN: Whittier public boat launch.

INFORMATION: Alaska State Tourism Bureau, P.O. Box E, Juneau, Alaska 99811, tel. (907)465-2010.

RESERVATIONS/ACCOMMODATIONS: Hotels at both Whittier (rustic) and Cordova. Reservations advised.

GUIDES/RENTALS/SHUTTLES: Prince William Sound Kayak Center (called The Rental Room in off-season), 2205 E. Tudor Rd., Anchorage, Alaska 99507, tel. (907)562-2866. Boat shuttle and full kayak rentals at Whittier from May 15 to September 15.

CAUTIONS: Glacier winds, glacier icefall waves, icebergs, high tides, bears, rain, oil tankers and other ships.

LOGISTICS: Kelley Weaverling publishes a kayaker's map of Prince William Sound showing a selected number of routes and campsites with handy information on the back. Available for $7.95 from Orca Books, P.O. Box 1308, Cordova, Alaska, tel. (907)424-5305. The chart for western Prince William Sound is NOAA chart 16700.

Going Outside: Chichagof Island, Alaska (pp. 29-39)

LOCATION: 75 miles west of Juneau, Alaska.

SEASON: May through August; best June and July.

TRIP LENGTH: at least 9 days. July is usually the best month for clear days.

DEGREE OF DIFFICULTY: Intermediate with expert accompaniment.

GETTING THERE: By air to Juneau or Sitka. Alaska ferry from Bellingham, Washington, or Prince Rupert, British Columbia, will take hard-shell kayaks to Sitka, Juneau, Hoonah, or Pelican: Alaska Marine Highway System, P.O. Box R, Juneau, Alaska 99811, tel. (800)642-0066. Charter floatplane: Channel Flying, Juneau, tel. (907)789-3331; Sitka, Mountain Aviation, tel. (907)966-2288.

PUT-IN: Pelican is the closest northern put-in; Sitka is the southern put-in.

INFORMATION: Alaska State Tourism Bureau, P.O. Box E, Juneau, Alaska 99811, tel. (907)465-2010.

RESERVATIONS/ACCOMMODATIONS: The U.S. Forest Service cabin at White Sulphur Hot Springs can be reserved through the regional Forest Service office (reservations should be made months in advance).

GUIDE SERVICE: Spirit Walker Expeditions, P.O. Box 122H, Gustavus, Alaska 99826, tel. (907)697-2266.

CAUTIONS: Open ocean coast with frequent storms, rainfall, and fog. Bears on main island.

LOGISTICS: The Alaska ferries make this one of the most easily accessed wilderness traveling destinations for hard-shell kayaks. See NOAA charts 17322 and 17321.

The Knife's Edge: The Queen Charlotte Islands, B.C. (pp. 41-51)

LOCATION: 80 miles west of Prince Rupert, British Columbia; 350 miles from Vancouver, British Columbia.

SEASON: May through September 15; best in May for wildlife.

· ACCESS GUIDE ·

TRIP LENGTH: 2 weeks one way, 3 to 4 weeks for a round-trip.

DEGREE OF DIFFICULTY: Intermediate.

GETTING THERE: By air from Vancouver, B.C., to Sandspit in the Queen Charlotte Islands. By water, take the B.C. ferries from Port Hardy on the north end of Vancouver Island and/or from Prince Rupert to Queen Charlotte City; tel. (604)386-3431. Air Charter: Trans-Provincial Aviation, tel. (604)637-5355. Boat shuttle and/or rental: Kevin Newton, Blue Heron Hostel, tel. (604)637-2345; Kallhin Expeditions, tel. (604)559-4746.

PUT-IN: Kayakers can put in from a dock adjacent to the ferry landing at Queen Charlotte City, or find a car shuttle to Moresby Camp via the interisland ferry, 25 miles south, or hire a boat or plane shuttle.

INFORMATION/RESERVATIONS: British Columbia Office of Tourism can provide basic information, tel. (800)663-6000. All visitors to Haida village sites must register with the Haida Gwaii Watchman's office in Skidegate, P.O. Box 609, Skidegate, Haida Gwaii (Queen Charlotte Islands), Canada, V0T 1S0, tel. (604)559-8225, or the Parks Canada office at Queen Charlotte City, tel. (604)559-8818.

GUIDES: Ecosummer Expeditions, 1516 Duranleau St., Vancouver, B.C. V6H 3S4, Canada, tel. (604)669-7741.

CAUTIONS: Sudden northwest winds off the crest of South Moresby Island can rip through the inlets on the east side. Caution is advised when making the open crossing to Ninstints.

LOGISTICS: Ideal trips are to circumnavigate Moresby Island (for experts only) or round-trip on the east coast of Moresby Island from Queen Charlotte City to Ninstints and back. Plan to spend a month. See Canadian Hydrographic Service (CHS) chart 3853.

Orca: Johnstone Strait, B.C. (pp. 53-63)

LOCATION: On the north side of Vancouver Island, British Columbia, 150 miles northwest of Vancouver, B.C., and 295 miles from Seattle.

SEASON: Mid-June through October; best July through September.

TRIP LENGTH: Allow 6 days for viewing the whales and the territory.

DEGREE OF DIFFICULTY: Beginner to advanced. Leaders should be familiar with strong tides and standing waves.

GETTING THERE: By car from Vancouver, take the B.C. ferry from either Tsawwassen or Horseshoe Bay to Nanaimo, Vancouver Island, and go north on Highway 19 to Port McNeill. Flights go twice a day from Vancouver International Airport to Port McNeill (Canadian International or Air Canada). From Seattle, Kenmore Air has scheduled seaplane service as well, tel. (206)486-8400. A bus shuttle runs from Port McNeill to Telegraph Cove (19 miles) 5 days a week for $5 per person. Taxi is $25 per load.

PUT-IN: Telegraph Cove has a boat launch and provides parking for nominal fees.

ACCOMMODATIONS: Port McNeill has several hotels and motels that tend to be crowded during the summer. There is a campground at Telegraph Cove.

INFORMATION AND RESERVATIONS: British Columbia Office of Tourism, tel. (800)663-6000. Port McNeill Tourist Information and Reservations, tel. (604)956-3131.

GUIDES: Northern Lights Expeditions paddles Johnstone Strait from June into September. Contact them at 5220 N.E. 180th St., Seattle, WA 98155, tel. (206)362-4506.

CAUTIONS: Blackney Pass and Weynton Passage have tidal currents in excess of 10 knots. Use the Canadian current tables and pass through at slack. Johnstone is a wind tunnel with particularly active storms from the southeast. At all times, watch out for ships when crossing major channels. Camping in Robson Bight is against the law. There are a few campsites along the Vancouver Island shore midway between the bight and Telegraph Cove. They can be very crowded in the summer—plan trips for early or late summer. Stay in this area briefly, and plan to tour the rest of the region, which has more campsite options. Noseums, the diminutive stinging insects, haunt most camps, especially along the Vancouver side of Johnstone Strait.

LOGISTICS: Keep a plastic bag handy in case a friendly fisherman offers a salmon. The B.C. ferries leave on time, and there can be a wait on Friday afternoons. See CHS chart 3456.

Point of Contact: Nootka Sound, Vancouver Island, B.C.
(pp. 65-73)

LOCATION: At the mid-point of Vancouver Island's west coast, 150 miles northwest of Vancouver, B.C.

SEASON: May through September; best in August through September.

TRIP LENGTH: 4 days.

· ACCESS GUIDE ·

DEGREE OF DIFFICULTY: Beginner to expert.

GETTING THERE: From Vancouver by car, take the B.C. ferry from either Tsawwassen or Horseshoe Bay to Nanaimo. Drive north on Highway 19 up the east coast of Vancouver Island to Campbell River, then west on Highway 28 through Gold River to the dock on Muchalat Inlet. The *Uchuck III* departs at 8 A.M. every Monday/Wednesday/Friday from late May through the summer. Call for reservations, tel. (604)283-2515. You can paddle Muchalat Inlet, also; start early because of the afternoon winds.

INFORMATION: British Columbia Office of Tourism, tel. (800)663-6000; B.C. ferry information, tel. (604)386-3431.

ACCOMMODATIONS: Gold River has motels, and a good campground is located on the highway midway between the town and the dock.

CAUTIONS: There are numerous reefs along the outer coast north of Friendly Cove.

LOGISTICS: Expect a 5- to 6-hour drive from Nanaimo to Gold River. It would be good to have a hand-held VHF radio if you intend to return on the *Uchuck III* and need to make contact; contact can be made through the lighthouse crew at Friendly Cove as well. The food and crew aboard the *Uchuck III* are excellent. See CHS chart 3664.

South Fork: The Skagit River Estuary, Washington (pp. 75-85)

LOCATION: 60 miles north of Seattle, 88 miles south of Vancouver, B.C.

SEASON: Year-round; best in mid-May, September.

TRIP LENGTH: Day trip.

DEGREE OF DIFFICULTY: Beginner.

GETTING THERE/PUT-IN: From Highway I-5, take the Starbird exit 218, which is 1 mile south of Conway, go west to the road's end, and cross the railroad tracks. There's parking along the river road past the boat launch.

INFORMATION: General information on the Skagit estuary is available from the Washington State Department of Wildlife, tel. (206)775-1311.

ACCOMMODATIONS: Lodging is available at numerous bed-and-breakfast establishments and motels in the area. Call Northwest Washington Tourism for information, tel. (206)221-TOUR.

GUIDES/RENTALS: Northwest Outdoor Center, 2100 Westlake Ave. North, Seattle, WA 98109, tel. (206)281-9694.

CAUTIONS: Make sure the outgoing tide does not leave you stranded on the tideflats. Take care to note the characteristics of the slough you have paddled as you enter the bay, if you intend to return the same way you came. Avoid the estuary during spring and winter floods when flood warnings are in effect.

LOGISTICS: Bring a bird book, binoculars, camera, and drinking water. Plan to stop at an isolated cedar stump to "blind-up" for lunch and watch the natural activities. Bring knee-high boots; in summer, try going barefoot. See topographic maps for La Conner and Utsalady.

Shi Shi: The Olympic Peninsula Seashore, Washington (pp. 87-95)

LOCATION: Northwest corner of Washington state's Olympic Peninsula, 150 miles from Seattle.

SEASON: Year-round. Best in the summer, for clear days and almost-warm water.

TRIP LENGTH: At least 3 days.

DEGREE OF DIFFICULTY: Expert. In summer, intermediates with surf-experienced experts.

GETTING THERE/PUT-IN: From the Seattle area, take the Washington state ferry from Seattle to Bainbridge Island or from Edmonds to Kingston, tel. (800)464-6400. Take highway 305 or 104, respectively, to join Highway 101 north past Port Angeles. Then take Highway 112 north to Neah Bay. Follow the main road west through town, and go south following the Air Force Base signs for 2 miles. Cross the Waatch River bridge, heading south, and stay right. Makah Bay is 1.5 miles from the bridge, the first good put-in. The second put-in is 1.7 miles beyond the first; stay right, cross the Sooes River, and go to the long beach. Watch for the last beach access before the hill. Travel time: 2 1/2 to 3 hours driving plus a 40-minute ferry crossing. There are long ferry waits on summer weekends. Trailer traffic is heavy on Highway 101.

INFORMATION: Olympic National Park, tel. (206)452-4501.

GUIDES/RENTALS: Northwest Outdoor Center teaches surf skills at Makah Bay every summer: 2100 Westlake Ave. North, Seattle, Washington 98109, tel. (206)281-9694.

CAUTIONS: In winter, high tides and rough seas can make beach landings impossible. Surf is higher on the northern end of Shi Shi Beach. Take great care around the arches. Fog is frequent in the summer. Bring a tide book and carry a VHF radio or good weather radio for weather reports.

· ACCESS GUIDE ·

LOGISTICS: Due to car vandalism, it's advisable to leave little gear in the car. The last house at the top of the hill past the second put-in will take care of your car for a nominal fee per day. In winter, be prepared for rain—bring extra tarps and knee-high boots. There are good campsites in the trees along the beach margin past Petroleum Creek. Carry your water in or purify water from Petroleum Creek. See topographic maps for Cape Flattery, Makah Bay, and Ozette.

Embayments: Willapa, Coos, and San Francisco Bays (pp. 97-107)

Willapa Bay, Washington

LOCATION: Washington state, 124 miles southwest of Seattle.
TRIP LENGTH: Day trip.
DEGREE OF DIFFICULTY: Beginner.
GETTING THERE/PUT-IN: By car from Seattle, go south on Highway I-5 to Highway 101, west to Highway 12, west to Highway 107, south to Highway 101, and south past South Bend to Willapa Bay. Look for put-ins near the highway.
INFORMATION: The Pacific County Museum in South Bend can provide information about the region, tel. (206)875-5224.
ACCOMMODATIONS: Southwest Washington Tourism, tel. (206)423-8400.
CAUTIONS: The mud, and getting stranded by the outgoing tide.
LOGISTICS: The quieter you are on this trip the more you'll see. Bring knee-high boots, and a big bag for muddied things on return. See NOAA chart 18504.

Coos Bay, Oregon

LOCATION: Oregon, on the southcentral coast, 215 miles southwest of Portland, 510 miles north of San Francisco.
SEASON: Year-round to Charleston, May through August is best including going outside to Sunset Bay.
TRIP LENGTH: Day trip to 3 days.
DEGREE OF DIFFICULTY: Beginner.
GETTING THERE: Coos Bay can be accessed along the Oregon coast by Highway 101. Driving south on I-5, take Highway 38 to Reedsport and go south to Coos Bay. Driving north, take Highway 42 to Coos Bay.

PUT-IN: The Coos River has few put-ins or take-outs and its banks are muddy. For the South Fork access, follow Highway 101 south through Coos Bay to Bunker Hill, going left to Eastside over the bridge and left through Eastside following the arterial. Cross Catching Slough going east and follow the Coos River along its south bank, following signs to Dellwood. Watch for the county boat launch signs roughly 10 miles from Eastside. Shuttle by cab is inexpensive. The best take-outs are just past the Highway 101 bridge on the south bank at the public boat launch on the northeast end of the Coos Bay airport runway. This take-out is without a phone; having a VHF radio would allow you to call the marine operator on Channel 25 for a taxi. Charleston harbor boat launch has all the amenities. If you go out the bar, south around Cape Arago is Sunset Beach, a safe surf landing. There's a pay phone at the park camping area entrance.
INFORMATION: Oregon State Tourism Bureau, tel. (800)547-7842.
ACCOMMODATIONS: There are numerous inexpensive motels and an excellent state park system. Sunset Bay State Park west of Charleston is one of the best paddling parks on the coast.
CAUTIONS: Avoid the river during periods of heavy rainfall in winter and spring. Bar conditions are at their worst during afternoon ebb tides. Stay clear of big ships under way in the channel.
LOGISTICS: The Coos Bay Pilot's Association Tide Tables, P.O. Box 2543, Coos Bay, Oregon 97420, tel. (503)267-6555, are invaluable sources of maritime information as well as taxis, weather, and bar condition, tel. (503) 888-3102. See NOAA chart 18578.

San Francisco Bay, California

LOCATION: San Francisco Bay, from the Marin Peninsula to San Francisco's Aquatic Park.
SEASON: Year-round.
TRIP LENGTH: Day trip.
DEGREE OF DIFFICULTY: Intermediate to expert, depending on wind and tide conditions.
GETTING THERE/PUT-IN: From San Francisco, take the Golden Gate Bridge going north. Take the Sausalito exit to Fort Baker, and find the small harbor at the base of the bridge's north pylon.

INFORMATION/RESERVATIONS/ACCOMMODATIONS: California State Tourism Department, tel. (800)862-2543

GUIDES/RENTALS: Sea Trek, 85 Liberty Ship Way, Sausalito, California 94965, tel. (415)332-4457.

CAUTIONS: Around the bridge, there are strong wind gusts, tides, and eddylines. Strong afternoon winds combined with an outgoing tide can be risky. Heavy ship and boat traffic.

LOGISTICS: There are sea lions around Fisherman's Wharf. Ask for your latté in a cup instead of a glass. See NOAA chart 18649.

Gunkholing: The Oregon and California Coasts (pp. 109-19)

The Lost Coast, Northern California

LOCATION: Northern California, 50 miles south of Eureka. From Seattle, 630 miles; from San Francisco, 325 miles.

SEASON: May to August.

TRIP LENGTH: 27 miles from Mattole Beach to Shelter Cove, 1 to 2 days.

DEGREE OF DIFFICULTY: Expert.

GETTING THERE/PUT-IN: Take Highway 101 to Highway 1, and go through Ferndale, south to Petrolia, then west to the Mattole River mouth.

INFORMATION/RESERVATIONS/ACCOMMODATIONS: County park camping.

CAUTIONS: Expect wind, strong currents, and fog. Drivers use low gear on downgrade into Shelter Cove.

LOGISTICS: Water available. Shuttle time from Shelter Cove to Mattole River one way: 3 hours.

Heceta Head, Oregon

LOCATION: Mid-point on the Oregon Coast, 181 miles southwest of Portland, 171 miles north of the California/Oregon border.

SEASON: May through September.

TRIP LENGTH: Day trip.

DEGREE OF DIFFICULTY: Intermediate to expert, depending on the weather and surf.

GETTING THERE/PUT-IN: Highway 101 to Devil's Elbow State Park.

INFORMATION/RESERVATIONS/ACCOMMODATIONS: Oregon State Tourism Department, tel. (800)547-7842.

CAUTIONS: Do not enter the Sea Lion Caves. The ocean conditions are active.

LOGISTICS: The park closes at sunset.

Cape Meares, Oregon

LOCATION: Northern Oregon Coast, 80 miles west of Portland.

SEASON: May through September.

TRIP LENGTH: Day trip.

DEGREE OF DIFFICULTY: Intermediate to expert, depending on sea conditions.

GETTING THERE/PUT-IN: Highway 101, or from Portland via Highway 8 to Tillamook. Follow the signs to Oceanside, and put in at the town beach.

INFORMATION/RESERVATIONS/ACCOMMODATIONS: Oregon State Tourism Department, tel. (800)547-7842. The closest campsite is at Cape Lookout State Park below Netarts.

CAUTIONS: Open ocean conditions.

LOGISTICS: The offshore rocks are a sensitive environmental area and a National Wildlife Refuge—no trespassing. The extensive beaches of the Tillamook bar may be accessed for hiking from the Cape Meares loop road. See NOAA chart 18558.

Anacapa Crossing: The Santa Barbara Channel Islands, California (pp.121-29)

LOCATION: The Santa Barbara area of Southern California, 60 miles northwest of Los Angeles.

SEASON: Year-round. March is known for strong winds and great wildflowers. There's the least wind in late summer, with the best conditions in September.

TRIP LENGTH: 26 miles to and from Anacapa Island. Minimum 3 days, 4 days would be excellent. There is a strong possibility of being stranded on the island due to high winds.

DEGREE OF DIFFICULTY: Expert.

GETTING THERE/PUT-IN: Highway 101 to Oxnard. Head west to Victoria Avenue, take a left, and head south along the east side of Channel Islands Harbor to a park locally known as Hobie Beach just south of the Coast Guard Station.

INFORMATION/RESERVATIONS/ACCOMMODATIONS: California Tourism Department, tel. (800)862-2543. For kayaker's information contact California Kayak Friends, 14252 Culver Drive, A-199, Tustin, California 92714. For required Anacapa and Santa Rosa islands camping reservations, contact Channel Islands National Park headquarters, 190 Spinnaker Drive, Ventura Harbor, California 93001, tel. (805)644-8262. Although there are limited campsites, there are frequent last-minute cancellations.

GUIDES: Southwinds Sports Resource, 1088 Irvine Blvd. #212, Tustin, California 92680, tel. (714)730-4820.

CAUTIONS: Be prepared for fog, northwest winds, short, steep seas, and ship traffic. The current, nicknamed the "rotary," can reach a speed of 2 knots and is unpredictable. High-speed recreational boaters use the same course as kayakers. Visually check for landmarks on the outbound leg, to aid on your return. A compass is a necessity. In the sea caves, wear a helmet and exercise extreme caution.

LOGISTICS: The National Park Service plans to have a paddle-in campsite area on the east end of Santa Rosa Island by September 1990. Pack in your own water, and carry out your trash. Park your car in the neighborhood, not at the park. Bring two 50-foot lengths of rope, two 18-foot lengths of webbing tied in loops, and two caribiners to rig a heavy lift system at the Anacapa dock.

The Translucent Sea: Baja California and the Sea of Cortez, Mexico (pp. 131-41)

LOCATION: Mulegé, on the east coast of Baja California in the Mexican state of Baja California Sur, 615 miles south of Tijuana.

SEASON: October through May.

TRIP LENGTH: From 5 miles south of Mulegé, 75 miles to Loreto. Plan 10 days to 3 weeks or more. (Note: in Chapter 11, we stopped short of Loreto and were picked up by friends.)

DEGREE OF DIFFICULTY: Intermediate.

GETTING THERE/PUT-IN: By air to Loreto and bus north to Mulegé. By car from the San Diego area, take Highway 1 south to Mulegé. Put in on any beach where campers congregate, and inquire about a safe place to park your car. A suggested place is the Hotel Serenidad, 2 miles south of Mulegé.

INFORMATION/RESERVATIONS/ACCOMMODATIONS/GUIDES: Call your local Mexican consulate. Trudy Angel has been guiding this route for 14 years. Contact her at Paddling South, 4510 Silverado Trail, Calistoga, California 94515, tel. (707)942-4796 (summertime), (707)942-4550. The

National Outdoor Leadership School has 2- and 4-week expeditions throughout the winter: P.O. Box AA, Lander, Wyoming 82520, tel. (307)332-6973.

CAUTIONS: By car, take a full 10-gallon gas can across the border and buy gas whenever you can below San Quintin. Use extra-grade gas, because lower octane gas can damage your car's catalytic converter. Gas is least available between Santa Inez and Guerrero Negros. The highway has been improving steadily, but drive with extreme caution. Most important: do not drive at night because of cattle on the highway. Paddling: always strive for a pre-dawn start to make distance. Carry as much water as possible.

LOGISTICS: Tourist permits are required and can be obtained at the nearest Mexican consulate or at the border (have your passport or a copy of your birth certificate with you). Gas up, change money, and buy Mexican car insurance—for the days you will be driving only— from drive-in booths in San Ysidro, California. Water is available at Mulegé; plan for three quarts per day per person. Charts are sketchy in detail. The Mexican topographical maps are best: the 1:250,000 series G12-5 map gives a good overview; the 1:50,000 topographical maps G12A-57, -67, -68, -78, and 88 give route details. Contact the Map Center, 2611 University Avenue, San Diego, California 92104, tel. (619)291-3130. Order well in advance of departure.

Mangrove Mañana: La Manzanilla, Mexico (pp. 143-53)

LOCATION: The state of Jalisco on the Mexican west coast, 100 miles south of Puerto Vallarta.

SEASON: November to January.

TRIP LENGTH: Base camp paddling, 5 to 10 days.

DEGREE OF DIFFICULTY: Beginner.

GETTING THERE/PUT-IN: Fly either to Puerto Vallarta or Manzanillo and take the bus to La Manzanilla.

INFORMATION/RESERVATIONS/ACCOMMODATIONS: Contact the nearest Mexican consulate. Beach camping or palapa rental.

GUIDES: Outback Expeditions, P.O. Box 16343J, Seattle, Washington 98116, tel. (206)932-7012.

CAUTIONS: Sunshine. Take care in the passes through and around the Churches Islands. Bury your valuables in the sand when away from camp.

LOGISTICS: If you are on your own, depend upon the bus system. If you intend to stay over at a resort, try Melaque 20 miles south or Manzanillo 30 miles south of that.

GLOSSARY

◆

Aleuts — the people of the Aleutian Islands in Alaska who, grouped with the Koniags of Kodiak Island and the Chugach of mainland Alaska, depended on the kayak for their livelihood.

arroyo — the channel of a dry stream; a deep, dry gully.

baidarka — the word used by Russian explorers and fur traders for the Aleut kayak.

Beaufort scale — a method of equating wind velocity and wave conditions at sea to a numbered scale from 0-12 and a word description. In Chapter 10, for example, force three (7 to 10 knots) is described as a gentle breeze that will create large wavelets and scattered whitecaps. Force five (17 to 21 knots) is termed a fresh breeze with moderate waves taking a more pronounced, long form, with many whitecaps, and some spray.

bivouac — a temporary encampment, usually without shelter.

breakdown kayak — a kayak whose frame and fabric skin most closely resemble the original Aleut and Eskimo skin boats. Often called a portable or folding kayak, these boats are best for remote journeys necessitating backpacking or air travel.

broach — when a boat is turned sideways to the direction of the wave. In sea kayaking, usually caused by being caught in breaking surf.

cabrilla — a rockfish of the bass family common to Mexican waters.

ceviche — a traditional Mexican appetizer of raw fish marinated in lime juice, garlic, and salsa.

chine — the break between the side and bottom of a kayak's hull. Kayak designers speak of a "hard" or angular chine offering crisp handling and a "soft" or rounded chine giving uniform stability.

close-hauled — a sailing term for when a vessel is sailing as close to the wind as she will go.

coaming — a raised frame around holes in the deck of a boat (as around a hatchway) to keep out water.

Escape — a high-volume, hard-chine kayak designed in 1980 by Mariner Kayaks in Kirkland, Washington.

Eskimo roll — a kayaking technique of righting oneself when capsized, by a sweep of the paddle and a snap of the kayaker's hips.

Feathercraft — a folding or breakdown kayak designed in Vancouver, British Columbia, made with aircraft aluminum, hypalon rubber, and Cordura fabric.

feathered — when a kayak paddle is fixed or adjusted in such a way that its two blades are opposed or set at a ninety-degree angle to each other. This allows the paddle blade to "knife" the wind on a forward stroke and minimize resistance.

ferry glide — also called ferrying, a method of kayak navigation for crossing currents by paddling on an upstream angle to counter the force of the current while your forward progress actually takes you laterally to your destination.

Folbot — a beamy, high-volume breakdown kayak of laminated wood and rubberized canvas made by Folbot of Charleston, South Carolina.

force three, force five — see Beaufort scale.

Gel-coat — a common sea kayak construction process that produces a finished outer coating of pigmented fiberglass resin that is bonded to the hull and can chip with hard contact.

hard-shell kayak — any rigid, nonbreakdown kayak.

hole-in-the-wall arch — an arch created by waves refracting around both sides of a headland.

hypothermia — the loss of mental control and body function due to prolonged exposure to cold temperatures.

kayak — (as used in *The Hidden Coast*) a sea kayak that is large, long, and built for long-distance open-water travel, as opposed to the low-volume, highly maneuverable river or white-water kayaks.

Kelty — a well-known backpack especially popular in the 1970s.

lee — the opposite side from that against which the wind blows; the side sheltered from the wind.

Nautiraid — a French folding or breakdown sea kayak designed before World War II and made of laminated wood framing and a rubber-coated fabric skin.

pogies — mitten-shaped gloves for kayakers; they have an open palm to provide a sure grip which is velcroed to close over the shaft of the paddle.

Polaris — (Polaris II) a medium-volume sea kayak designed by Dan Ruuska, who is known for his excellent workmanship and outspoken support of sea kayaking.

portage — the act of carrying boats and gear overland from one body of water to another.

· GLOSSARY ·

serac — a large block or tower of ice created as a glacier flows and fractures down an incline or overrides an obstruction.

spray skirt — a skirtlike garment made of waterproof coated nylon and/or neoprene which fits around both the kayaker's chest and the coaming of the kayak, making the cockpit watertight.

surfing — when sea kayakers utilize the slope and forward motion of a breaking wave to ride their kayaks at an accelerated rate of speed.

survival suits — full-body dry suits required for overwater flight on most helicopter sorties during the *Exxon Valdez* oil spill.

Thermarest cushion — a self-inflating seat pad or sleeping pad made by Cascade Designs of Seattle, Washington.

wave train — "trains" or groups of waves created by ocean swells as they travel from their source. Though an imperfect science, when surf landing, kayakers will watch the wave train for a pattern and then follow the biggest waves in.

Wind Dancer — The name of a sea kayak made by Eddyline Kayak Works that is known for its stability.

Zodiac — an inflatable breakdown or folding boat powered by an outboard motor that is especially useful at fly-in destinations.

BIBLIOGRAPHY

◆

Angell, Tony, and Kenneth C. Balcomb, III. *Marine Birds and Mammals of Puget Sound.* Washington Sea Grant Publication. Seattle: University of Washington Press, 1982.

Arima, E. Y. *The West Coast (Nootka) People.* Victoria B.C.: British Columbia Provincial Museum, Special Publication #6, 1983.

Baeger, Johann Jakob, S.J. *Observations in Lower California.* Transl. by M. M. Brandenburg and Carl L. Baumann. Berkeley: University of California Press, 1952.

Bascom, Willard. *Waves and Beaches.* Garden City, New Jersey: Doubleday, 1964.

Bent, Arthur Cleveland. *Life Histories of North American Birds, Marsh Birds.* New York: Dover Publications, 1963.

Brookman, Al, Sr. *Sitka Man.* Anchorage: Alaska Northwest Publishing, 1984.

Carefoot, Thomas. *Pacific Seashores, A Guide to Intertidal Ecology.* Seattle: University of Washington Press, 1977.

Caughman, Madge, and Joanne S. Ginsberg. *California Coastal Resource Guide.* Berkeley: University of California Press, 1987.

Chapman, Charles F. *Piloting, Seamanship and Small Boat Handling,* Vol. 5. New York: Motor Boating, 1963-64 edition.

Coyle, Jeanette, and Norman C. Roberts. *A Field Guide to the Common and Interesting Plants of Baja California.* La Jolla, California: Natural History Publishing, 1975.

Dabberdt, Walter F. *Weather for Outdoorsmen.* New York: Charles Scribner's Sons, 1981.

Dalzell, Kathleen E. *The Queen Charlotte Islands.* Volume 2: *Places and Names.* Queen Charlotte City, B.C.: Bill Ellis Publisher, 1981.

Davidson, Art. *In the Wake of the* Exxon Valdez. San Francisco: Sierra Club Books, 1989.

Dowty, Karen Jones. *A Visitor's Guide: The California Channel Islands.* Ventura, California: Seaquit, 1984.

Duffus, David A. "Non-Consumptive Use and Management of Cetaceans in British Columbia Coastal Waters." Unpublished dissertation. University of Victoria, British Columbia, 1988.

Dyson, George. *Baidarka.* Edmonds: Alaska Northwest Publishing, 1986.

———. "An Illicit Alliance—The California Sea Kayaking Boom of 1803-1841." *Sea Kayaker* 4:1(Summer 1987):8-14.

Howorth, Peter C. *Channel Islands, The Story Behind the Scenery.* Las Vegas: KC Publications, 1982.

Hugill, Stan. *Shanties from the Seven Seas.* New York: E. P. Dutton & Co., 1961.

Ince, John, and Hedi Kottner. *Sea Kayaking Canada's West Coast.* Vancouver: Raxas Books Inc., 1982.

Johnson, William Webber. *Baja California.* New York: Time-Life Books, 1972.

Kirkendall, Tom, and Vicky Spring. *Bicycling the Pacific Coast.* Seattle: The Mountaineers, 1984.

Krause, Aurel. *The Tlingit Indians.* Translated by Erna Gunther. Seattle: University of Washington Press, 1956.

Krutch, Joseph Wood. *Baja California and the Geography of Hope.* San Francisco: Sierra Club Books, 1967.

Lethcoe, Nancy R. *Glaciers of Prince William Sound, Alaska.* Valdez: Prince William Sound Books, 1987.

Lilly, Kenneth E., Jr., Cdr., *National Oceanographic and Atmospheric Administration.* Marine Weather of Western Washington. Seattle: Starpath School of Navigation, 1983.

MacDonald, George F. *Haida Monumental Art: The Villages of the Queen Charlotte Islands.* Vancouver: University of British Columbia Press, 1983.

———. *Ninstints.* Museum Note #12. Vancouver: The University of British Columbia Press in association with the UBC Museum of Anthropology, 1983.

McCall, Lynne. *California's Chumash Indians.* Rosalind Perry, ed. Santa Barbara: Santa Barbara Museum of Natural History, 1986.

Michaels, Leonard, David Reid, and Raquel Scherr, eds. *West of the West, Imagining California.* San Francisco: North Point Press, 1989.

Mickleson, Pete. *Natural History of Alaska's Prince William Sound and How To Enjoy It.* Cordova, Alaska: Alaska Wild Wings, 1989.

Miller, Pam. "Mangroves, On the Fringes of the Tropics." *Sea Kayaker* 6:3(Winter 1989-90):28-33.

Moziño, José Mariano. *Noticias de Nutka.* Iris Higbie Wilson, trans. and ed. Seattle: University of Washington Press, 1970.

· BIBLIOGRAPHY ·

Muir, John. "The Pacific Coast Glaciers." In *Harriman Alaska Expedition Series,* in cooperation with The Washington Academy of Sciences. Edited by C. Hart Merriam, Vol. 1, 1902.

Northern California Atlas and Gazetteer. Freeport, Maine: DeLorme Mapping Co., 1988.

Pacific County and Its Resources. South Bend: Pacific County Board of Commissioners, 1909.

Paz, Octavio. *Selected Poems of Octavio Paz.* Bloomington: Indiana University Press, 1968.

Peck, Cyrus E., Sr. *The Tides People, The Tlingit Indians of Southeast Alaska.* Juneau, Alaska: Juneau School District Indian Studies Program, 1975.

Peterson, Emil R., and Alfred Powers. *A Century of Coos and Curry.* Portland: Binfords and Mort, 1952.

Peterson, Lester R. "British Columbia's Depopulated Coast." In Howard White, ed., *Raincoast Chronicles First Five.* Madeira Park, B.C.: Harbour Publishing, 1976, pp. 156-63.

Pethick, Derek. *The Nootka Connection, Europe and the Northwest Coast 1790-1795.* Vancouver, B.C.: Douglas & McIntyre, 1980.

Pilot Chart of the North Pacific Ocean PILOT558807. Washington, D.C.: The Defense Mapping Agency, July-September 1988.

Pilot Chart of the North Pacific Ocean PILOT558904. Washington, D.C.: The Defense Mapping Agency, April-June, 1989.

Pyle, Robert Michael. *Wintergreen.* Boston: Houghton Mifflin, 1986.

Robbins, Chandler S., Bertel Bruun, and Herbert S. Zim. *Birds of North America.* New York: Golden Press, 1966.

Spong, Paul. "The Whale Show." In *Mind in the Waters,* Joan McIntyre, ed. New York: Charles Scribner's Sons, 1974.

Steinbeck, John. *Log from the Sea of Cortez.* New York: Penguin Books, 1986.

Stewart, Hillary. *The Adventures and Sufferings of John R. Jewitt, Captive of Maquinna.* Seattle: University of Washington Press, 1987.

Swanton, John R. *Contributions to the Ethnology of the Haida, The Jesup North Pacific Expedition,* Vol. 5. New York: The American Museum of Natural History, 1975 (a reprint of the 1905 edition by E. J. Brill, Lieden and G. E. Stechert, New York).

Thompson, Richard E. *Oceanography of the British Columbia Coast.* Ottawa, Ontario: Department of Fisheries and Oceans, 1981.

U.S. Fish and Wildlife Service, "Total Marine Birds Retrieved Following the *Exxon Valdez* Oil Spill," U.S. Fish and Wildlife Service, Anchorage, December 19, 1989, quoted in Art Davidson's *In the Wake of the* Exxon Valdez. San Francisco: Sierra Club Books, 1989.

Van Arsdell, John. "B.C. Whaling: The Indians." In Howard White, ed., *Raincoast Chronicles First Five.* Madeira Park, B.C.: Harbour Publishing, 1976.

Warshall, Peter. "The Ways of Whales," In Joan McIntyre, ed., *Mind in the Waters.* New York: Charles Scribner's Sons, 1974.

Washburne, Randel. *Kayak Trips in Puget Sound and the San Juan Islands.* Seattle: Pacific Search Press, 1986.

Washington Atlas and Gazetteer. Freeport, Maine: DeLorme Mapping Co., 1988.

Weyler, Rex. *Song of the Whale.* Garden City, New York: Anchor Press/Doubleday, 1986.

Wood, Charles E. *Charlie's Charts of the Western Coast of Mexico Including Baja.* Surrey, B.C.: Charlie's Charts, 1968.

Woodbridge, Sally B., and John M. Woodbridge. *Architecture, San Francisco, The Guide.* San Francisco: 101 Productions, 1982.

INDEX

· INDEX ·

· INDEX ·

Many other fascinating books are available from Alaska Northwest Books™.
Ask at your favorite bookstore or write us for a free catalog.

Alaska Northwest Books™
A division of GTE Discovery Publications, Inc.
P.O. Box 3007
Bothell, WA 98041-3007
1-800-343-4567